LEUKEMIA AND KEY LIME PIE
(SIMPLE PLEASURES)

MATTHEW M.W. MORRELL

Published by Big Earth Publishing
923 Williamson St.
Madison, WI 53703

ISBN 1-890768-77-4

THE FOREWORD, IN KEEPING FORWARD...

"Never underestimate a man with nothing to lose, as a man with nothing to lose is a dangerous man." Late summer, 2005, Madison, Wisconsin. This was the line Matt Morrell posted to lure his enemy. With bite, bravery, and balls, Morrell was pacing the hallways of his body—with a flashlight in one hand and a Smith and Wesson in the other—bullying, baiting, hunting down the very goddamn thing that came to trespass. A 28-year-old intellectual jock jailed to a hospital bed. This was not the plan. This was never his life. I'm too young. I'm too healthy. If God has a sense of humor, tell him to stop using me as a punch line. I'm sick of this joke. I'm sick of seeing doctors. I'm sick of being pitied. I'm sick of being sick. These beds, these walls, that smell. I never made this reservation. This bed is for old people, really sick people, busy tubes and empty toe tags; people occupying St. Peter's lobby while waiting around for judgment. I'm not supposed to be here. I don't even believe in all this.

So down the hallway he goes, like a panther with spurs, donned in a dusty hat and badge, saddling up the Tombstone of his bloodstream. So what does cancer look like? How does cancer smell? Can you taste cancer? Does cancer make a sound? Can you kill cancer?

The following pages are an account of Matt Morrell's hospital stay, written from his bed as he sat in waiting. An expensive purgatory with a staff. His notes on family, friends, expectation, hospice, leukemia, sports, life, love, living, and the unavoidable are scribed in this truth. They are simple pleasures to say the least. These 80 plus entries are a testament to Matt's understanding and acceptance. But even acceptance can still scream, "Horseshit!"

Matt Morrell is a good friend of mine. Tough, passionate, smart, competitive, loyal, brazen, unsettled, tenacious, honest. I'd wager any one of his friends has felt this entire cocktail at one time or another. His family, even more. We met in junior high school, struck up a strong friendship in high school—both blue-eyed Irish Catholic boys who gave the finger to religion and expected nothing in return. Jameson became the drink, and to be drunk became the magic. I doubled his words, but he said more, he meant more. A salute to our differences is how we met in the middle. Jameson was our referee, and the whiskey normally won. "Irish luck," Matt would say. I agreed.

Matt's circle is a unique place to pull up a chair. Armed with wit, and anchored in honesty, you can't fool, trick, or dodge the man. He just wants you to be you and nothing else. Bring your game, but don't get silly. If he wanted to befriend actors he would've gone to Hollywood. All he really wanted in friendship was authenticity, a genuine smile, and a true rapport enveloped with laughter and good times. He does not open that door for just anyone, but once you earn his trust, he'll hold that door open for a lifetime. You know it when you're there, that door, Matt at the entry, beer in hand, a smoke and a smile. The sense of something good always came with this combination.

Matt's whirlwind began in October of 2001. Diabetes came first, followed soon by a beat up liver, where the cirrhosis was so advanced, Matt was placed on an immediate transplant list. Then came the Leukemia. Chemo followed more chemo and remission was celebrated. It was back to golf, work, flirting with law school and a future best served healthy.

I think it was Muhammad Ali who said, "My way of joking is to tell the truth. That's the funniest joke in the world." Ali was Ali, the 'Louisville Lip' who has rung the bell a few times with his own inner war, his own locked-in punch with fate. A smooth roar emanates from this champion. Anger flooded with sadness. The same cry courses through Matt. Both shadow boxing with themselves. The fight in the fighter, champions in every respect; to win the rounds, but still hold your breath for the decision. The truth of this matter was becoming awful, hard to digest, a reality easily forgotten when you heard the sound of Matt's laughter. We are reminded the strong are victims too. Spring 2005, "Is it me again?" Matt asks. A man in a white coat answers, "I'm afraid it is." Matt swallows his pride and perhaps a tear. "Is it back like before?" The man responds, "It's worse."

Late summer, 2005, Madison, Wisconsin. Diagnoses transplant: bone marrow. Matt's cagey ego crawling on the walls, his reserved humility a medical rap sheet, a personality tailored to cross-checks and floating 20's to friends in need. He waits for science, the optimism from others, the blood from his brother—tired doesn't even begin to explain his severe exhaustion. He goes on, he writes, he learns to adjust, again. Waiting, waiting—it can get pretty hard, lonely, boring in this penalty box. Months add up, they pile like rotten leaves. October always made Matt nervous. Wicked memories from this harsh month. Bad news seemed to arrive like the chills. Am I doing this for me or for others? How much can I really take? My body looks like a pale bruised-up apple, I'm connected to tubes and machines, I have to wear a mask in public, I take 4 naps a day and fists full of pills when I'm awake. My mind still kicks a little ass and I appreciate that. I haven't had a drink in two years. I'm drunk on sickness, smashed on insurance forms, high on something called hope, except the only thing I feel is the hangover. No good parts in this night. My stories are very sober. Am I doing this for me or for others? I was supposed to be dead years ago. I'm living now. This is living. This is living? The news comes again. It's inevitable. It rears its ugly head again like the ravenous cancer it is. Apparently its hungry for more and here I am ... the perfect host, the unlucky address. "I never let you in! I NEVER LET YOU IN!! You never knocked you bastard, you just came through the door and made a mess of my house. This is trespassing! Trespassing goddamn it! THIS IS STILL MY HOUSE!"

Back down the hallway, with the flashlight and Smith and Wesson. The cancer scurries, scratches, stains and steals. It avoids the flash of light Matt sends down its way. It hears the sound of boot heels and metal, Matt's revolver and silver bullets. It loots, it robs, it wants to kill. This was a dirty fight to begin with. A stacked deck riddled with aces and eights. Where the gallows are high, and the rope is loose. Both Matt and I know cancer will hang for this. High noon, big crimes, mortality our common thread. This fight will continue, but this fight is hard. This cancer does not want to make Matt a living witness. The graffiti is black, shows on his biopsies, his blood counts, his everything.

This 2-year man hunt has made Matt a desperate sheriff, with a loving posse of friends and family ready for swift justice.

Some fights exhaust the piss and vigor from their very essence. This fight knocked Matt right on his ass, but he didn't care for the view. Up off the ropes, blood in his eye, swollen and almost shut—but when you hear the bell you still come out punching. Hard medicine, my friend. He remembers the arena, he remembers his friends and family, he remembers why he's billed to fight, but he can't make out his enemy. Things got blurry, silhouetted against the fear, hidden in the howls of his hallway, with a wail and the scream, that beastly cry only a sick man hears when he's face to face with wrath. Where the hell are you? Where are you hiding? You reappear and disappear and reappear like a bad habit. Show your face and let's fight just once in the open and be done with it. Why can't I find you? Don't you know you're killing me? Or do you know you'll never go away until I close my eyes for good? I'm right here goddamn it. I'm right here! Fuck You! Fight Me!

"Never underestimate a man with nothing to lose, as a man with nothing to lose is a dangerous man." Matt, you're still dangerous. You'll always be dangerous. A son, a brother, and a friend. Lightning in a bottle, the echo of a great shotgun. Matt, you'll always be up for the fight no matter where that fight takes you. Fists clenched, chin up, eyes narrowed and clear. Your corner is stacked with love. Courageous and tough, some of us shouting out cheers, some of us holding back tears. Keep fighting Matt—for when you turn around, just know, your corner will always be here.

R.S. Praefke
January/2006

POSTSCRIPT:

A life rare in length, rarer in impact. It's been about a month since we lost Matt. The reality seems harder now, the absence bigger. March Madness and baseballs opening pitch seemed to fall flat this season. The competitive spirit gone, the meaning different. Anger, sorrow, confusion still abundant. The preceding foreword was written with Matt's approval, when rage and possibility were still the weapons of choice. However, acceptance was creeping toward reality. A tough reality you wanted to kick in the teeth. You could feel it then. The preparations had a finality to them. Aiming for eternity with sand, glass and gravity keeping time.

Matt Morrell was dignity to the very end. Quick and wide smiles, hand-breaking handshakes, that wink and laugh, his voice clever and smart, quietly shouting affection, in confidence, in conversation, in silence, with humility and honor, dignified and very human. He had the knowledge of knowing. He found the simple pleasures in life from that knowledge. "Leukemia and Key Lime Pie" was written out of that knowledge, that hope, but understood by his fate. He never let that doom make pity of his case. He rose above things most of us will never face. Dignity to the very end. Somewhere now in a new beginning.

We all want our friends to be great teachers, strong with trust, original of thought and firm in pride. The following journal is a mountainous reflection of the man some of us were lucky to know. He was all those things, and more. Courage to the core, vulnerable too, a family man and friend, a poet armed with honesty and mend, just getting to that place first where we'll all see each other again. He knows. Someday we'll all know.

I can see him now, somewhere in this cosmic adventure, pulling up a chair at that big poker table in the sky, watching Matt pass the cards around, with his black hat and filled cup, dealing that next round, breaking another deck, telling us where we really go after we sin. He'll know. I think he's always known. That was his gamble, that was his game, and knowing my friend the way I do, if you're playing against him, he'll still find a way to win.

Your deal Matt.

R.S. Praefke
April/2006

THE MEDICAL BACKGROUND:

Matthew M.W. Morrell, known to many as "Relli," is a 28-year-old 1995 graduate of Neenah High School and 1999 graduate of Eastern Michigan University. Matthew has been battling several illnesses the past three and a half years.

While previously battling Type-1 Diabetes and Advanced Cryptogenic Liver Cirrhosis, Matthew was placed on the liver transplant list in June of 2003. He was taken off the liver transplant list in October of 2003, when he was diagnosed with Acute Myelogenous Leukemia. After undergoing two rounds of induction chemotherapy and two rounds of consolidation chemotherapy, Matthew was considered in remission in April of 2004.

However, in April of 2005, Matthew's leukemia relapsed and he again was diagnosed with Acute Myelogenous Leukemia. He was advised that his only chance for a cure to his leukemia is a bone marrow transplant.

Matthew is now preparing to undergo a bone marrow transplant in which his twin brother, Mark Morrell, will be the living donor.

A NOTE FROM MATT'S MOTHER:

It has been a whirlwind, the past week! Words cannot truly express what the heart feels when you experience a day like Sunday, August 21st. Thanks to all who contributed to make Matt's benefit a reality! Thanks also to all who attended and to all who were with us in spirit. But most of all, thanks to you, Matt, for your courage to continue on your journey! The inspiration you left us with will be remembered by all who listened to you speak as we accompany you on your way ...

Matt will begin writing from here on out until he is unable to do so. I've asked Matt to consider sharing his awesome message on his caringbridge site for all who were unable to hear him last Sunday.

Matt's journey continues; a new chapter begins today. He will check into University of Wisconsin Hospital this morning and begin a five day round of chemotherapy which will prepare him for the actual transplant scheduled to take place on Tuesday, August 30.

Mark too, is preparing to begin his rounds of two injections per day which will stimulate his stem cells for the extraction process which will take place on Monday, August 29.

Thanks again to all of you for your love and support! Stay tuned for Matt's updates ...

Helen Morrell

MATT MORRELL'S SPEECH DELIVERED THE NIGHT OF HIS BENEFIT:

I would like to take a couple moments to say a few personal thank you's to the following people who have made this unique day possible. First off I would like to thank Waverly Beach and Keith Jorgenson for hosting and working with us on organizing this event. I would like to thank Leroy and his wife for providing the sound system for the bands and I would like to thank the bands "Level", "Half Empty", "The Mitch Rivers Band", "Little Missy", and of course, "Vic Ferrari", who have donated their time and talents to provide today's outstanding entertainment. I would like to thank all the nurses and doctors who I have had the fortune of working with on my journey and a special thanks to those of you who are personally in attendance. I would like to thank my girlfriend's family for their help and support and I would like to thank my girlfriend Amy, who has so admirably and lovingly put up with me during every step of this ordeal, which has definitely not been the easiest task to take on. I would also like to thank my father, my mother, my two brothers and their wives and my relatives for their love and support and the roles they played in today being possible. I would especially like to thank my mother who has spearheaded this benefit and took what was simply just an idea and turned it into a reality that has been presented here today. I would also like to thank every individual and business who is represented on the three dynamic posters located around the benefit. There is a reason those names are displayed and my individual thanks will never be enough, but yet all that I have. And lastly for now, I would like to thank all of you who are in attendance today in support of my family and me. The outreach of support and well wishes has been extremely overwhelming in the most precious of ways and is a direct correlation in today being possible. My family and I will forever be indebted to each of you and the kindness you have bestowed upon us.

I'm sure by now, all of you here are well aware of my situation, so I'll simply just say that it's been a whirlwind of emotions, changes, choices, and decisions that I would not wish upon anyone. Unfortunately, life does not work that way and we are forced to make decisions and deal with the reality of our situations. That however, can be a very trying time, as some decisions in life ultimately decide our future. It is in those choices that one truly finds out who they are and what they are capable of.

In October of 2003 when I was first diagnosed with leukemia, I was given one of these choices. I was politely told that the human body trying to fight three major diseases through a lifetime is not so easily accomplished. Trying to fight three major diseases within a span of two years however, would explain the reason I was given a choice along with my treatment options. I could go home and let the fire inside of me burn out or I could try to add gasoline. I was given less than a 10% chance to survive and forty two days after treatment started, I walked out into the most beautiful December day that there will ever be and came home. My battles, decisions, and choices however, were far from being over and far from being easy.

Through out the past few years, I am constantly hearing how proud people are of me, how I am an inspiration to others, and how good I look for what I've been through. I answer these compliments with responses of "you should not be proud of me because you would make the same decision", that "I am not an inspiration, but rather a person inspired by those who have already gone down the road I am on", and lastly, that "I always look good"!!

In all honesty, it simply comes down to a choice and a quote from a very humble man. As anyone who is a sports fanatic knows, the first ever ESPN ESPY Awards was presented in March of 1993 and an award was presented to Jimmy Valvano, a man who knew he was going to die from cancer. After accepting the "Arthur Ashe Award for Courage", he gave a speech that still sends shivers down my spine and makes the hair on my arms stand straight up. At the end of his speech, he said that he had one last thing to say. And I quote, "Cancer can take away all my physical abilities. But it cannot touch my mind, it cannot touch my heart, and it cannot touch my soul". Those twenty five words are why I am here today, why I have faced each obstacle presented to me, and why I am still trying to play golf with a catheter hanging out of my chest!!

Unfortunately though, my ability to make decisions and choices came to a screeching halt this past April when my leukemia relapsed. I was only able to make the choice to go through with another battle against leukemia because of a different choice. That choice that was made is the real reason why all of us are gathered here today. I may be under the heat of the spotlight, but the real spotlight deserves to be gracefully upon my twin brother Mark. Mark, without your willing choice to be my living bone marrow transplant donor, I do not have the chance to chase my dreams, I do not have the chance to see the places in the world that I haven't seen, and most importantly, I do not have a chance to live. Because of your choice, now I do. And I thank you for that chance and will never be able to truly express my gratitude for your choice. Thank You.

Thank you all once again, and enjoy the rest of your evening.

WEDNESDAY, AUGUST 24, 2005 10:02 PM, CDT
A JOURNEY THROUGH BLUE

There is nothing I can say about what occurred on Sunday, to justify what it truly meant. To all of you who attended the benefit, my sincere thanks … thank you for the feeling of hope and support through the day and for taking time out of your lives to share a moment with my family and myself. To those who made the day a reality … my sincere thanks. To those of you who are visiting the site and posting messages … they help me through the day. Feel free to leave more than one message and ask questions if you do not understand what I have written and I will try to clear it up for you. Medical jargon is now one of my fortes, so maybe we will all learn something new!!

What follows is simply a small taste of what a nonablative stem cell transplant (from here on out noted as a "mini") for a person with my conditions entails. What I know, experience, and learn will be shared. Enjoy.

Matt

WEDNESDAY, AUGUST 24, 2005 10:30 PM, CDT

I have been asked by numerous people to post my speech from Sunday. To honor those requests, I tried to post the speech on this site. However, journal entries are limited to 5000 characters and no HTML postings, which means copying my "word" document on a laptop that is outfitted with "works" and trying to paste on this website via this computer, doesn't work.

So … if I am not too busy lying around and killing time here in the hospital, I will retype the speech and post. Otherwise, I am more than happy to e-mail a copy of it to anyone who requests it. You can request via this site or I can be reached via e-mail at: Relli11@aol.com

Matt

WEDNESDAY, AUGUST 24, 2005 11:29 PM, CDT
DAY ONE

Today I awoke and began a journey that has taken nearly four months to begin. There have been numerous hospitals and physicians unwilling to attempt this "mini" transplant due to my situation and therefore, I am very grateful to Dr. Mark Juckett and everyone on the bone marrow transplant team here in Madison, who have given me the benefit of the doubt. All anyone asks for in their lives is a chance—thank you.

Amy and I arrived at the hospital at 10:45 a.m., I was admitted, and then sent to outpatient lab for initial blood tests. An hour later, we were on the way up to my "cell without bars" and I was given one of the worst rooms on the floor, that was small, claustrophobic, and a view with one tree in a small courtyard surrounded by red bricks, because the unit was full. That didn't sit so well with me and three hours later, a room opened up and I had a view of the State Capitol in the summer sky and owe a thanks to my nurse Christi, who made the change possible and helped me move into a larger "cell without bars".

I then unpacked my stuff as I refused to earlier and have settled nicely into my room. I met with Linda (My Nurse Practitioner for my stay) and Dr. Juckett. I signed my consent forms, went over a few items, and discussed the plan of attack.

Chemo began at 6:17 p.m. on the dot and I was disconnected at 6:52 p.m. I was given the chemo of Fludarabine, which is given in doses of 30mg per meter squared. I am just a bit less than 2 meters squared, so it was a dose of just under 60 mg. I also began the daily drugs of Fluconazole, Acyclovir, Sulfa, and Pantoprazole. Lorazepam and/or Dolestron is used for nausea and I have a nightly "cocktail" of Oxycodone and Benadryl to ease the constant pain and aches in my bones and to get a decent nights rest … Cont.

WEDNESDAY, AUGUST 24, 2005 11:52 PM, CDT
DAY ONE CONT.

I will receive five days of Fludarabine and on days four and five, will also receive Cytoxan. There are other things to also be started later, but will advised of that when they occur.

The rest of the night was spent watching the Little League World Series, Mythbusters, and flipping through summer TV. That reminds me of another event that took place on Sunday—the end of "Six Feet Under" on HBO. I had a chance to watch the finale on Monday and I sure hope there are some other fans of the show, as I would like to know what you think of the ending … I thought it was simply brilliant. The music jammed so hard, that I went out and got the CD at Best Buy on Tuesday. Brilliant … wish I could watch the last 5-10 minutes again right now!!

Anyway … one small step taken forward today and I'm confident in my decision.

Matt

THURSDAY, AUGUST 25, 2005 11:19 PM, CDT
DAY TWO — PROBLEMS ALREADY!!

Thursday began as any usual day in the hospital—I am trying to sleep as late as I can in the morning, with plans to "wake up" just before "Days of Our Lives" starts. Now I know what everyone is thinking, but "Days of Our Lives" in the hospital kills an hour and is easy on the eyes. My plan begins to be foiled early though, as I am woken up constantly from 6:30 a.m. to 10:00 a.m. to be weighed, to be given my pills, to have the janitor clean, to speak to the physical therapist, to talk to the dietician, to let my nursing assistant Jane know that I'm not ready yet to have my sheets changed, and finally to speak with a member of the diabetic team assigned due to being a transplant patient. I finally get a clean hour of sleep from 10:00 a.m. to 11:00 a.m. and there is a knock at the door—I reply "Yes, I will eat breakfast when I wake up" and slowly get up out of bed and make the 6 step trip to my resting chair!!

Anyway—Christi (RN) came in shortly before noon and was surprised to see me awake. "It's nice to see you finally up", I believe were her exact words. (I have become used to this nice chiding from my morning nurse staff long ago and believe they secretly like having me as on of their morning patients because they know they won't have anything to do!!) Jane (NA) came in shortly after and was happy to finally be able to change my sheets!!

After "Days of Our Lives", I went through my morning routine of getting ready for the day, drinking an energy drink (which by the way can be stocked up on at Big Lots for 48 cents a piece), and taking my first walk. I have not yet figured out a walking pattern here in Madison, but took a nice stroll around the front grounds to get some fresh air and to feel a bit of normalcy. As I came back into my room, I met Dr. Dixon who is part of the diabetic team following me. I was relieved to hear him say that I would be allowed to use my insulin pump, as my HA1C is at 4.7, and that is better than some healthy people, so he made my day. I usually have to cut through the "red tape" to be able to manage my own diabetes and glad once again that I won the battle. Matt 7 and Hospital Policy 0. Small victory but they all help!!

Anyway—although my day had been going smooth and normal, it wasn't to be. I found out late this afternoon that both of my Hickman Catheter (HC from now on) lines are infected with a gram positive bacteria. I am a-symptomatic, meaning that I am showing no signs of infection, even though bacteria is living inside the plastic lines of my HC. The bacteria does not require oxygen to live, so is therefore able to exist in my lines. I received this news from Linda (NP) and she advised that Dr. Juckett would make the final call on what would happen, but that they may have to remove my HC. This is not a positive step for me, as then everything would have to be done peripherally or through the veins on my arms. Chemo and transplants are ideally done through an artery as opposed to a vein, so that is the problem. They need more time to grow the cultures to find out exactly what type of infection it is, but I am a bit awestruck that I have no symptoms of a functioning bacteria—things never cease to amaze me sometimes!! (As of 11 p.m. tonight, I have not heard anything as for what they have decided to do, so I am anxious for tomorrow).

After I found out the above news, they started to treat me immediately with Vancomycin or simply Vanco. This will take one hour to infuse and will be every 12 hours until they know how to treat the infection. About 30 minutes after the start of the Vanco, I experienced what they call "Red Man Syndrome" and reacted to the medicine. My body flushed red, I heated up, and I have never itched so terribly in my life. They slowed the rate down and from now on, I will be pre-medicated and the Vanco will run over two hours. Woohoo.

Day Two of Fludarabine was given at 6:00 p.m. and ended just short of 7:00 p.m. Nothing new learned from that time to know, so I will consider Day Two over. I didn't think that this procedure would run according to plan and was expecting certain complications down the road. However, my road extended past Day Two, but at least I learned something new in that my body doesn't like Vanco and that taking impeccable care of a catheter does not guarantee a healthy catheter. The "joy" of learning from experience never gets old!!

SATURDAY, AUGUST 27, 2005 12:35 AM, CDT
DAY THREE—FREEDOM!!

My day began way too early this morning when I was hooked up to my Vanco antibiotic at 4:00 a.m.—at least I was given a benadryl and there was no "red man syndrome", so at least that is a positive!! Later around 8:00 a.m. labs were drawn out of my catheter and Dr. Juckett and Linda came in to discuss the infected HC. They are waiting to see if the bacteria has colonized yet or not. What is meant by that, is that the bacteria will form in one spot creating a wall or a colony—a basic build up. The hope is if that is the case, to be able to break through that wall and destroy the bacteria via the Vanco. I also leaned that bacteria will attach itself to the HC line inside of me and will "colonize" and at some point, will break through and enter the

HC line. That is their thought on how it may have gotten infected, but its all a guessing game. So—just playing the waiting game for now and hoping I don't "crap" out on the first roll of the dice.

Stacey (RN for the day shift) was glad to see that I rolled out of bed around 11:40 a.m. so that she could make my bed—they sure are quick on changing your sheets around here!! I went through my same morning routine and after "Days", took a walk. Today however, I felt like I hiked to Guam and back. I was gone for an hour walking around the back of the hospital, taking in the sites, and ending up on University Avenue. I won't try to explain where that is if you aren't familiar with the area, but I'll simply say it was a long walk and I wasn't where I thought I was. So—I turned around and walked the same way back and ended up finding my way into the hospital on the first floor near the cafeteria—note to self—explore in car only!! Then I made it back up to my room around 2 p.m. and had brunch.

SATURDAY, AUGUST 27, 2005 12:37 AM, CDT
DAY THREE—FREEDOM CONT ...

(Keep forgetting I only get 5000 characters per posting).

This afternoon, I had an interesting experience. I had a knock on my door this afternoon and two people came into my room. One was named Laura and I can just recall the other woman as Mom. Apparently Dad was in for a bone marrow transplant in the room I can see out of my window. Well we chatted for a few minutes and they said they had read the article in the Post Crescent and thought it looked like me, so they came over to check!! Apparently they are from the Appleton area and also were followed at the Martha Siekman Center, but we haven't seen each other there. But—we started talking about AML cause that is what the Dad has and his transplant is next Friday. His sister is going to be the donor and she was the only match out of five or six brothers (can't remember) and four sisters. Anyway—they left and about a half hour later the Dad came in and introduced himself as Bill. Well we started chatting and I came to find out that his wife (Mom) has colon cancer and is going to be treated down here in Madison also while Bill (Dad) is going through the transplant and their daughter (Laura) is going to be here to take care of both of them. Anyway—its kind of weird to be told "hey—I know you from the newspaper" and I am just amazed on how many people are coming into contact in my life just because of this terrible disease. Its as if there is an instant bond just because you are going through the same situation. It's nice to know "the others" as to just hearing about "the others". But to my point—I ask that everyone who reads this, also takes this family into your prayers and well wishes, along with the Westphals, a family from Neenah whose son Corey is currently recovering from a bone marrow transplant and who I had the pleasure of meeting while down here in Madison in July. Small, small world in this cancer community I find myself in the middle of and how sad that it keeps growing.

But on to a more positive note, my Vanco was given at 4:00 p.m. this afternoon and Day Three of Fludarabine followed at 6:00 p.m. and was done at 7:00 p.m. At 7:15 p.m. this evening, I found myself sitting at the "Blue Moon" Bar with my friend Korn who drove down this afternoon!! They gave me a pass out of this place from 7:15 p.m. to 11:00 p.m. and Korn and I took full advantage. (Yes I know it is weird that I was let out, but my chemo is the easy part and my problems will come post transplant next Tuesday—so my free and "healthy" time is a miracle to me and I just keep a smile on my face and laugh at what I'm doing!!) I had a tasty bacon cheeseburger and fries and watched the Packers first half disaster. ("Blue Moon" gets 2 thumbs up from Korn and I, but I would recommend trying not to have the waitress who will dump your glass of water fully on your lap—at least Korn got a free drink out of my misfortune!!). Then Korn and I tooled around trying to learn some things about Madison and met his brother out at "Babes"—a Sportsbar that continued showing the New England game and had a corner with a band playing and a "Golden Tee". We played two rounds of "Golden Tee"—Korn won as usual—and then it was time for me to return to my "cell". As I returned at 11:15 p.m. (was supposed to be back at

11:00 p.m.) Katherine (NA) looked at her watch and looked at me and looked at her watch and said, "You're 15 minutes late". I replied, "Traffic in Madison at this time of night is just terrible". She just laughed, kind of how I was laughing for the past 4 hours—like a little kid in a candy store!!

SUNDAY, AUGUST 28, 2005 12:58 AM, CDT
DAY FOUR—CYTOXAN SUCKS

I'm listening to a band called "Lucero" right now and its extremely difficult to listen to them and type, as they just rock. I recommend any alternative / alternative country fans to visit their website—luceromusic.com—and give them a try. Every album they have is pure heart, soul, and guitar riffs that simmer in your head all day long—I find myself singing way too much as opposed to typing and I guess that's just me. They are finally making their way up near the Midwest on their current tour and will be playing in Chicago on Sept. 23rd (with a sweet new band called Limbeck) and I can't wait to be in the middle of that crowd, even if its with a mask on and a plastic bubble surrounding me. HA!

Anyway—what a long day today has been. My friend Kurt drove up this morning to pick Korn and I up for some breakfast, as I was allowed on leave after a 9 a.m. clearance check. We ended up at the "Hilltop Family Restaurant" which was okay—think the Pancake House would have been better, but we didn't want to wait in line. After eating, we took a drive back to my apartment and then we drove all around the south and west parts of Madison, finding how to get to grocery stores, a movie theatre, places to eat, Wal-Mart, and anything else that's necessary to know where it is located in the city. We did a nice job in the time we had and I don't think it will be too bad getting around.

We then returned to my apartment and tried out the ping pong table in the basement and then just chilled up in my actual apartment. Amy came into town around 3 p.m., which was just in time to take me back to the hospital. I was given my pre-med (Benadryl) and had my Vanco drip start at 4:25 p.m. and ended around 6:00 p.m. At that time, day four of Fludarabine began. They also started to fill my body with Saline Solution in preparation for the Cytoxan. What they ended up doing was giving me 1 liter of saline solution in an hour while the Fludarabine dripped in. They also gave me Dolsetran for nausea, which was going to be certain with the Cytoxan. The Fludarabine and Liter Solution ended about the time the NASCAR Race in Bristol, TN started. Damn Jarrett and Neuman having to play rough getcha later cowboys and wrecking my weekly fantasy pick of Harvick for nothing—I had a few choice words for both of those clowns and then cheered on my boy Tony Stewart to an 8th place finish in his backup. In fact, instead of calling Tony Stewart my boy, I might as well just start calling him the 2005 Nextel Cup Champion!!!

But back to real time now and the Cytoxan began at 7:11 p.m.—c'mon—7:11 p.m. like it was going to be good luck or something. I will tell you all something … I was ready and willing to take on Cytoxan, I did, and it kicked me straight to the curb. I was nauseous, my head became all stuffy, I got a headache, my nose ran, and I felt like I got hit by a two ton truck. The only side effect from Cytoxan that I didn't get today was hair loss, but like that is a big deal right now and won't happen in two weeks anyway. Wow. I just got whooped. On top of that, after the Cytoxan was complete, I received another half liter of saline solution!! Good times—good times!! Amy sat with me the whole time and she just kept telling me I looked like I was tired and asking if I felt alright—rough two hours—.

Anyway—enough about me. I talked to Mark today and he is in the middle of his Neupogen shots and says they are kind of kicking him a bit too. He has been bothered with headaches and lose of strength and overall just feels like I do most days—which I think is good for him!!! (For a few days anyway!!). His daughter Madison is being baptized tomorrow and then he is coming down to Madison tomorrow night to be ready for his big day on Monday!!

So—that's all from here. One more day of chemo to get through and then I have a day off. I need a day off. In fact, I can't remember the last time I had a day off. So in all reality, its a good thing I have a day off then!! (I have always said—however I can justify it—simple pleasures—simple pleasures).

MONDAY, AUGUST 29, 2005 02:01 AM, CDT
DAY FIVE—CYTOXAN 2 MATT 0

As is customary, my morning began with a Vanco drip at 3:30 a.m. from my nurse Kim. She reminds me of a nurse I had at Froedtert named Julie. They are both close to my age and I think its a reciprocating relationship, as I can talk to someone my age and they can have a patient their age and that point of understanding where the other is coming from is easily known. Its nice.

Later a bit after 8:00 a.m., Dr. Juckett came in and we chatted for a bit. I found out that my gram positive bacteria is a Staph Infection (Staphylococcus to be exact). I happen to have the lesser of the two evils of a Staph infection and was informed that the Vanco should be able to take care of it. Blood will be taken tomorrow morning to be sure and I am confident that things will be okay.

We also went over the transplant. Mark's blood is O+ and I am B+. His blood does not have an antigen like mine, which means I won't recognize his blood/immune system, but his will recognize mine and go after it. At some point during the fighting (Immediately, three weeks, 6 weeks, etc) I will become jaundiced as this fight effects bilirubin levels in the liver. The hope is for it to happen later as opposed to earlier. If it happens earlier, my body is already compromised due to the chemo, so the chances of defending myself are less. It could turn my whole body against me and that would not be good. On top of that, I started the anti-rejections drug Tacrolimus today, which should start to increase bilirubin and liver enzyme levels, so being monitored for problems now becomes a major concern and priority.

And switch to some good news—I was given a pass again this morning and went with Amy to eat at the Original Pancake House, as Kramer, Korn and I didn't the other day. We waited about a half hour and then got seated. The place was phenomenal—anything you could think of for breakfast was served and I think we spent most of our time watching other people eat their food because it all looked so kewl and interesting!! Then we went to Star Cinema and watched "Four Brothers". I think John Singleton is a heck of a director and thought the movie was stellar—good car chases, good fight scenes, typical guy flick stuff!! Amy even enjoyed it, so that gives it props already. Then it was back to the hospital.

Here is where my day turns a bit sour. My Vanco had started at 4:30 p.m. and ended around 6:00 p.m. However during this time, I was witness to one of the best comebacks in Little League World Series history. Hawaii was up 1-0 over Curaco, who then scored three runs after just a poor, poor call by the umpire. So it was 3-1 Curaco. In the bottom of the 3rd, Hawaii bombs back to back homers to tie the game up at 3-3. In the 5th, Curaco sends a single and a double shot yard and take a commanding 6-3 lead, which holds until the bottom of the 6th. Hawaii starts with a walk in the bottom of the sixth, then a bloop double and then they squeeze bunt a run in to make it 6-4. A squeeze bunt—are you serious!! Then a base hit makes it 6-5, a walk loads the bases, and a ground ball ends up scoring a run to tie it up at 6-6. I couldn't believe what I just saw and was literally cheering for these kids from Hawaii in my room like I was at the game. Then Corporate America reared its ugly head and ABC went for the almighty dollar instead of showing what they had been for the past 2 1/2 hours. When the game went to the 7th, it was announced that the Pacific USA would see the rest of the game and all others would have to turn it on ESPN2 to catch the end. Well guess what—I don't get ESPN2 in the hospital and I threw a hissy fit. Do you know what ABC put on instead of showing the 7th inning—they put on an infomercial about a *$%@&()#@ fishing lure. A Fishing Lure. Are you @#$%^&* serious. I call for an immediate boycott of ABC. To pour salt in the wound, I have just learned that Hawaii won the game with a lead-off home run in the bottom of the 7th. Good thing I have the number for the best darn fishing lure ever instead. Steamed over that one

MONDAY, AUGUST 29, 2005 02:08 AM, CDT

But—Day Five of Fludarabine started around 6:10 p.m. along with a liter of saline. I also took the first anti-rejection tacrolimus pill. The Fludarabine ended about 7:15 and Day Two of Cytoxan began at 7:25 p.m. and after a half liter of saline, I was unhooked at 9:50 p.m. I didn't even try to take on cytoxan today, as I chose to sleep all the way through it, which only made me wake up feeling like I had my worst hangover since Ryan Praefke and I played the role of rock stars in Washington D.C. over labor day weekend nearly three years ago. Boy does that weekend bring a sly smile to my face!!

Anyway—I was given a three hour pass at 10:00 p.m. and Amy and I went to meet my parents at their hotel, as they had just arrived from driving in from Minnesota. We left the hotel to go to Denny's to grab some food and Cytoxan had a few uprising surprises for me, which I gladly let the lawn deal with. Oh well—as we arrived at Denny's, Mark and Michelle showed up, as they too were just arriving from Minnesota. They left after a few minutes to go get some rest after a long day and the rest of us had some late night breakfast!! Now I am back in the hospital and I am doing alright.

The best part of the day though, is that I am now done with chemo and still kicking. A few white coats advised me that I would not make it through the chemo. I just don't think there is any better feeling in the world than proving someone wrong after they told you it couldn't be done. Never underestimate a man who has nothing to lose, as a man with nothing to lose is a dangerous man.

PS—Thank you to everyone for your Posts. I read all of them everyday and for those wondering, Todd is going to waste his number 1 draft pick in Fantasy Football on Peyton Manning, which will leave him without a decent running back, meaning he won't make the playoffs. I already told him I would bet that my first and second round picks (9 and 16) will outscore Manning and his 24th pick—he's thinking about it—It was nice to hear from you Tommy—I hope you are doing well and staying strong yourself—and finally Mr. Mason—I will make a business deal with you and everyone visiting the site can be witnesses. If you find me a publisher, I will be more than happy to offer you co-rights and we'll go 50/50 right down the middle and I will include a finders fee of a round of golf at University Ridge!!

Fishing Lures over Baseball—that's going to bother me for some time.

MONDAY, AUGUST 29, 2005 11:48 PM, CDT
DAY 6—4.2 MILLION

This morning was a rather tough morning to begin ... I couldn't really seem to drag myself out of bed to fast as I felt a bit unstable and all I really wanted to do was get down by Mark to sit with him for his process. However, my parents came into my room about 10:00 a.m. and I was still zonked out and they let me know Mark began his process at 9:25 a.m. A few minutes after my parents arrived, so did Amy. At this point I finally was able to make it from the bed to the bathroom and I got ready for the day. Dr. Juckett and Linda came in a bit after 11:00 a.m. and just gave me a look over. My magnesium levels are low, so I am now on Magnesium tablets, which they said will kind of like being on Milk of Magnesia, so I don't need to go into detail on that. But they have decided that everything is fine with my infection and I will be receiving the transplant at 9:00 a.m. tomorrow through my HC.

So—Amy and I finally made it up to where Mark was about 11:30 a.m. or so. Amy said "HI" and then left to go back to Oshkosh in time for work and then Dad, Mom, Michelle, and I sat with Mark for about the last hour or so. I can't really describe the machine that was being used, so everyone will have to take a look at it when we post the picture on the site. Personally, I think it was just plain kewl. You were able to see the blood being separated inside the machine and see the blood coming out of Mark and into the machine and then back into Mark. The most important part however, was a salmon color bag hanging on the top, which was being filled with Marks

Stem Cells and is what I will be receiving tomorrow. The hope is they get enough stem cells in one try and for that to happen, they need between 2 and 5 million. We would later find out that they were able to harvest 4.2 million stem cells from Mark. 4.2 million!! So—Marks job is finished and although he was a bit sore and tired, should be just fine by tomorrow.

After Mark was done, we all went down to the cafeteria to have some lunch. So far this morning, I had thrown up once in my room and was unable to stomach anything. For lunch I tried a Diet Sunkist and a bite of a banana—a few minutes later someone kindly called for a cleanup in aisle three, as the bathroom was further away than it looked. After finally making it to the bathroom and leaving my mark, I took an indirect way around back to the cafeteria and announced it was time to go and that I needed to go home—sad to think I am calling an apartment in Madison home, but I guess right now it kind of is.

TUESDAY, AUGUST 30, 2005 01:45 AM, CDT
DAY 6—4.2 MILLION CONT …

My parents dropped me off at my apartment around 2 p.m. and then they woke me up five hours later to say they were hear to pick me up for dinner. Boy did I need those five hours!!

After we decided where to eat (Boston's Gourmet Pizza and Restaurant), Mark and I went back inside the apartment to get a map so we could find our way there. We started talking a bit and I jokingly said to him, "How does it feel to know that tomorrow you might just kill me?". He said, "Well at least I will finally get some revenge against you!" and we both started to laugh and put our arms around each others back and then I said, "You know that whatever happens, you need to know that it isn't your fault". He said that it had been on his mind, but he was okay. To hear that calmed my fears that he would hold something against himself and I'm glad he is able to differentiate. Some people in life cannot and I'm happy he can!!

We all then went to Boston's to grab some supper. We ordered a Mushroom and Cheese Pizza for Michelle and Mom and a Mamma

Meatza for Dad, Mark, and I. When our pizza arrived, Mark started to inspect it and then I tried a small bite of it and had to swallow it with my soda. I said it tasted like goulash that we were forced to eat as kids and we all started laughing, but my mom was a bit flabbergasted as she thought her goulash was good, but I can say Mark and I never like it!! Dad was also only able to stomach one piece of pizza, so they made a new one for us with original sauce instead of goulash sauce and it turned out much better!! We then finished with a piece of Boston Creme Pie and a piece of Cheesecake for everyone to split except me, as I had to have my own piece!! I'm a big fan of Boston Creme Pie!! After supper, my parents dropped me off back to the hospital just in time for curfew!!

Anyway—in less than 9 hours I will be going through a bone marrow transplant. I have always said I would do anything once, twice if I like it. I guess I never thought that would include a bone marrow transplant though—Tomorrow I go to war. Its the first time in my life that I am going into battle with hoping I don't win, as if I do, it won't be good for anyone. To be brutally honest I am excited and scared as hell. But I am at peace and that's important. I don't think anyone is truly prepared for anything in their life, but that ones preparedness is judged on how they react to the situation the are faced. Things happen and that's the true honesty of life. However, that doesn't mean we have to accept what happens in life. There is a very fine difference. I am lucky to be getting a second chance at life tomorrow and that's truly an amazing feeling. I ask anyone who is able to participate, to have a shot of "Jameson" wishing me the luck of the Irish and thinking this is one damn fine Whiskey. As our high school hockey team and infamous "purple" line used to huddle and shout before each game "1,2,3 Kick Ass"!!

WEDNESDAY, AUGUST 31, 2005 12:47 AM, CDT
DAY 7—SEVEN MINUTES

I was awoken this morning around 8:00 a.m. for preparation for the bone marrow transplant. I kind of just laughed. I let Hikmet (RN) set everything up and then she kind of just left me alone. I still wasn't feeling all that well and I kind of drifted off to sleep until about 8:45 a.m. or so. Shortly after waking up, my Dad, Mom, Mark, and Michelle arrived and we all just sat around waiting, with the room kind of full of a nervous / happy energy.

Just shortly before 9:30 a.m. Dr. Juckett, Linda, Hikmet, Dr. Tim (I don't know his last name but we always talk about golfing), and a student nurse entered with what is going to become my new bone marrow. I am now clear and free of any ongoing investigations that involve my DNA, as today it has changed!! Now I can finally go back to Oklahoma with Casey!!

They double checked the stem cells as they do with any blood product and then Dr. Juckett hung the bag of promises and opened up the line and the stem cells started to drip in. I had chills and just kept staring at the bag, watching it drip into me. I glanced once at my mom and dad in the corner, who were being handed a box of kleenex and decided to overt my eyes before I started. It took seven minutes. Seven Minutes. Nope, I am not kidding. Seven Minutes for the transplant to take place and the fighting to begin!! At 9:37 a.m. my new life began. But wait—it gets better ...

My vital signs had to be monitored for one hour post transplant and in that time, my brother Todd and his wife Sara showed up. Soon after that, they gave me a mask to wear and I was given another pass out of the hospital. Literally just over an hour post transplant, I was on the way to my apartment!! Even though I still felt terrible and spent the rest of the day sleeping at the apartment in between bouts of cleaning the toilet, the smile I couldn't show on the outside was definitely smiling on the inside and in my mind!!

My friend Todd and his girlfriend Chanin were at my apartment when we all showed up and before long, my family went on a mission of groceries and misc. items needed for the apartment. I visited with Todd and Chanin for awhile, watched Chanin have a blast picking vegetables out of the garden I have access to, and then had to let them leave, as the next four hours were nap / cleaning time!!

Tonight we all took care of some business and then went out to eat at Chili's, where I was able to stomach my first taste of food for the day—some chips and salsa, a bite of a turkey sandwich, and some spiced apples. Think a new born eats more than that, but that was a small victory for me. Small victories—they will now be my way to get through the days!!

I want to thank everyone for their e-mails, messages, and calls today. I haven't been able to get back to everyone, but know I appreciate it, as does my family. Tomorrow begins my second rejection drug of Methotrexate, which is in conjunction with the Tacrolimus, which is going to be something where the doctors are going to need to find the right dose to walk a very fine line, which could bring in some rough days. The easy part for me is over and the hard part begins. The next few weeks are important, as the studies doctors are relying upon are showing that patients with liver cirrhosis are not making it past two to three weeks post transplant. That is why it was so hard to find someone willing to attempt this and why my appreciation and respect lye very deeply with Dr. Juckett.

Today I joined another community of people—those people who have had the opportunity to receive an organ transplant. I call transplants opportunities because in reality, that is what they truly are. Opportunities to continue on down the road of life. Simply amazing—simply mind-blowing—simply a miracle.

PS: Thanks to Dave and Kristine Wiegman for planting the "Tree of Hope" today, Neenah High School for allowing it, and those who attended—To TK: Thanks for the Irish Blessing—To JHawk: Thanks for the DC memories of everything—To Korn and Burks: Good luck on your tour to find a bar in Neenah with Jameson—To Dan: We'll take that bet—To Everyone Else: Cheers!! And to my family who shared this day with me: Thank You.

I just had a bone marrow transplant—I don't think saying that is going to get old for quite some time!!

WEDNESDAY, AUGUST 31, 2005 11:01 PM, CDT
DAY 8—MOVING ON

I have come to believe that there are no better words to hear than, "You are being discharged". Four simple words that lift the spirit, add hope to the mind, and brings smiles to everyone who had watched your journey, from the doctors, to the nurses, to your family, and to your new best friend, the pharmacist.

This morning I was given my first dose of methotrexate, which will then be given on day 3, 6, and 11 post transplant. It is a type of chemo that is more of an immune suppression drug, as compared to a total wipeout of the system. After that was injected into me, my nurse Christie advised me that she heard a little rumor that I was being discharged today. I refused to believe her because my hopes have been dashed before, so I chose to stay in bed and fall back to sleep for a bit.

After about twenty minutes, the pharmacist on the floor came in with a daily medication list that I just looked at and laughed. Drugs here, drugs there, drugs everywhere!! Anyway—at this time I knew that I was being released from "my cell without bars but a hell of a view" and we went over my daily pill popage schedule. After he left, I jumped out of bed and began packing quicker than a rabbit running from a fox. I was in the middle of my stuff strewn everywhere when Dr. Juckett and Linda walked in. Dr. Juckett asked me, "If I was going somewhere" and I replied, "I think so!!".

My plan of attack is as follows: My tacrolimus level is at 7 right now. It needs to stay between 5 and 15 or it needs to be adjusted. They aren't really sure they have anything under control right now, so I will be going into the hospital everyday for at least the next two weeks for lab tests. I'm sure within a few days my counts will drop to where I need blood transfusions and platelet transfusions, but that should only last a week, compared to the six or seven it takes after I receive regular chemo. I'm still on magnesium which wrecks havoc on the bowels and begin taking Sulfa to prevent a rare type on pneumonia in bone marrow transplant patients around September 24th. Again—the next few weeks are crucial and even though they have let me escape, I am not out of the woods, as any sign of problem puts me back into my "cell". If I can start to get my immune system back up to strength before day 30 post transplant, I will have better odds to be able to fight off the Graft vs. Host Disease (GVHD from now on) that the doctor is hoping I receive at least a mild form of, as that is a sign of the transplant working. However, too much of a good thing can be bad also, so we will deal with that when the time comes.

Other than that, I was able to stomach two breadsticks and a piece of Rocky Rococo Pizza for lunch, which is the first meal I have kept down in two days. Dad, Todd, and Sara headed back to Minnesota after lunch and my mom dropped me off at my apartment, where I promptly spent the next four hours in a much needed rest.

Amy came up for the evening and we just watched "Sahara", which was a rather entertaining movie. However, my few hours up has now led to another round of trying out my "new bed".

I don't know which part of the day was better: Hearing, "You are being discharged" or replaying in my head, "You will never make it out of the hospital if we try this". Either way, they both bring a smile to my face, even if they are two types of smiles!!

FRIDAY, SEPTEMBER 02, 2005 01:01 AM, CDT
DAY 9—ATOMIC SURVIVOR

Sometimes I feel that I do more work in a day being sick, than I do when I actually put in a day of work, but I haven't done that in so long, I even forget what that is like!! I know what you may be thinking, but hear me out for a few minutes …

My day began at 7:00 a.m. as I need to shower and shave before leaving for the hospital at 8:00 a.m. Now you are thinking you can't be complaining about getting up at 7:00 a.m., but you would be correct. Getting up at 7:00 a.m. after popping pills all day and night for nausea, which for me double as sleeping pills, is like waking up after taking on the local tavern for an evening. Of course I have not personally experienced that feeling, but from what I have heard, I think I am making a fair comparison. Anyway—Mom, Amy, and I left at 8:00 a.m. and made the trek to the hospital.

Now the trek to the hospital turned out to be like fighting morning rush hour traffic, as the slick route I had found from my apartment to the hospital, turned out to be full of little kids and proud parents experiencing the start of school. Now I knew there were two schools on this route I so carefully dissected, but in no way did they figure into my thinking that they would ever present a problem. Note to self—find a new route. We finally arrived at 8:20 a.m. and made the our way up to what will now become a second home for the next few weeks.

We checked in and were immediately sent to a secure room away from people, as crowds of people right now are my main enemy and my defense of a duckbill looking mask, just needed to be taken off for a bit. We were put in a lab room at 8:30 a.m. and my labs were immediately drawn and my nurse for the day named Matty took my vitals and asked a few questions. Then we sat, and sat, and sat some more. Two and a half hours later, we were allowed to leave. However, waiting two and a half hours tends to wear on the patience, especially when you are hoping that every footstep you hear is your angel of mercy. The tasking and impatience on the mind, is like having to work for four hours straight with not being able to at least pull up the internet at work and check the box scores of last nights games.

But back on track, the labs came back and everything is as expected. White Blood Cell Count (WBC) is getting lower, platelets are stable at 42,000 (normal person has 160,000 to 370,000), liver enzyme levels are rising and my bilirubin level will soon turn me a dashing shade of yellow for a bit. The only worry was that my tacrolimus level was low and so they have increased that dosage to 2mg for tonight's dose and tomorrow morning.

After we left at 11:00 a.m., all I wanted was a cozy bed and a comfy pillow, but seen as Amy didn't want to go to Culvers, which is oh so close to home, we ended up driving out to Middleton to eat at "Quaker Steak and Lube", which could turn out to be the best decor restaurant I have seen. It had full size corvettes, NASCAR cars, motorcycles, framed pictures of anyone and anything, signs, poster girls, etc, etc. Seen as we were here and sitting in the booth furthest from human contact, I decided to make the most of it.

SHU is short for Scoville Heat Unit, which is the number of units of water it takes to make a unit of chile pepper lose all traces of heat. It takes 2500-5000 units of water to neutralize the heat from one unit of jalapeno or one jalapeno pepper. I bring this newfound knowledge to you because I wasted no time in becoming a member of the "Atomic Wings Survivor Club". I signed a release form (seriously) and then ate an "Atomic Wing", which has an SHU of 150,000. Just like taking candy from a baby. They gave me a bumper sticker and my name will proudly be displayed at the Quaker Steak and Lube's Wall of Atomic Wing Survivor's. You can expect to see my name on the board after October 15th, 2005 and so the bar has been set. Its all about the small victories in a day—small victories.

Anyway—it was then time for my lengthy afternoon nap and the rest of the night was spent watching "Sin City"—I like it.

So—if you see where I am coming from and give me the benefit of the doubt, my day of being sick is like working a full day!! And like everyone else, I must now get some sleep to wake up tomorrow morning and do it all over again.

Goodnight.

FRIDAY, SEPTEMBER 02, 2005 11:24 PM, CDT
DAY 10—I'LL TAKE THAT BET

I have concluded that every day I go in for lab results, is going to be a two to three hour event and the best way to approach this is to bring a good ole fashioned book along.

Today started the same as the past two, we made the same mistake of passing by two schools, which really doesn't make for a real difference in time, but I just hate sitting in a car not going anywhere. I would rather be driving for 15 minutes than driving for 10 minutes and sitting for 5. At least I feel like I am accomplishing something, but I guess that is just my lack for being able to sit still. We made it to the hospital at the same time and went in for labs at the same time and left at the same time. The only difference is that I also received my second injection of methotrexate, which for some reason I had to tell them about, as it wasn't in my chart at the labs and the orders were, according to my nurse, "lost in cyberspace". Well its a damn good thing I wasn't "lost in cyberspace" too or someone would have had something up their something after I had my something up their something, which probably wouldn't have been a good day for that someone, so it's a good thing I was really on earth today. Counts dropping as expected and blood and/or platelets may be needed tomorrow or Sunday. Liver enzymes holding. Everything else seems to be okay.

So other than that, today was pretty uneventful. Except as we left the hospital, Amy spilled Gatorade on her shirt and then five minutes later noticed she was sitting in butter in the back of the car. That was after Mom was wearing her cup of coffee on her shirt at the hospital, but before I dropped my buttered roll that made a mess in three places on my pants, but not before mom spilled BBQ sauce on her shirt. If you followed that you can imagine the jokes made and repercussions handed back out. Also, Amy left this evening to make it back for a long weekend of work and then school starting on Wednesday.

Now I'm not one to make a bet or play cards without putting something on the line, as I'm sure you are all familiar with, and it just so happened today was my day. As we turned down Fish Hatchery Road to find Tony Roma's to eat lunch at, my mother said she bet that it was on the left hand side of the road, therefore wanting to merge into the left lane. I took that bet for lunch that Tony Roma's was on the right side of the road, earning us a stay in the right hand lane. Now seen as I had this bet won when Mom made it, it was hard for me hide the smile of knowing I was going to have a full rack of ribs for lunch and they couldn't have tasted better, especially when the bill came. Thanks Mom.

On top of that, my friends Korn and Kramer came down for a visit and we played a friendly game of Texas Hold Em for a $5 ante. Kramer started on fire and soon thought his A/9 would beat an all in of Korn's pair of 10's, pre-flop. They didn't. Then Korn thought his full house after the Turn was enough to beat my present two pairs. However, after I bet $1000 after the flop and he raised to $3000 which I called, he then only bet $1000 after my check on the flop, which I matched. This in turn led to the river being a 9, therefore making my two pairs into the top full house draw, which led to my all in which Korn called and was flabbergasted to see. So—thanks for coming down boys and paying for dinner.

So all in all, two bets, two free meals, and two more reasons why its always worth it to roll the dice

SATURDAY, SEPTEMBER 03, 2005 10:55 PM, CDT
DAY 11—SETTLED

Well, today I finally unpacked all my bags and officially "moved in" to the apartment. Looks a tad more comfortable than bags and crap strewn everywhere.

The doctor was the same—blood and platelets dropping and other counts holding steady. Am betting that I will need platelets tomorrow, as I am at 23,000 today and believe they will transfuse under 20,000. Not sure though, as some prefer to transfuse under 15,000 and some prefer under 10,000. So I guess that is something I will have to ask.

Pretty boring and uneventful day though, which are the days that are what I need right now until my counts come up. Expect it to be this way for the next week or two. I did take Korn and Kramer down in a game of hold em again before Kramer finally broke my winning streak in the second game. Sometimes you have to lose just to make sure they come back!!!

On a side note, I don't have ESPN or ESPN2, but you can still listen to the games if you can put up watching scrambled TV or having it in the background. Just isn't the same, but I will just have to do with what I've got!!

Boring days bring boring journal entries, but at least we can all look forward to the "RACE" tomorrow at California in prime time on NBC!! There go the simple pleasures again!!

SUNDAY, SEPTEMBER 04, 2005 11:11 PM, CDT
DAY 12—A NEW RECORD IS SET

After the past few days thinking of new ways to kill time while at the hospital for labs, I decided to bring in my laptop today and continue the preparation for my Fantasy Football Draft on Tuesday, where Todd has now changed his mind and is thinking of taking

Priest Holmes—then he will have to waste a pick on Larry Johnson cause Holmes will go down, so I am glad Todd is in my division and I get to play him twice!! But much to surprise, just as I had everything setup and ready to roll, Hikmet (my nurse) came in and said I was good to go home. I laughed. She was serious. I laughed again. She was still serious. My counts had held through the night and my platelets were at 21,000, only a 2,000 drop from Saturday. So—I didn't need a transfusion (found out its under 20,000 as I am used to), my hemoglobin was holding at 9.0 (transfusion under 8.0), and my tacrolimus level had risen back to 5. My White Blood Cell Count is dropping and was at only 400 (means I am seriously neutropenic and susceptible to serious infections, which I'm not a fan of). But even more thrilling than that news, was that it only took 45 minutes. 45 Minutes. Nice day to catch a break!!

Again—a relatively uneventful day. The downs included watching Syracuse vs. West Virginia—what a terrible game—it was like watching my hair grow. I had a two hour fight with my bowels and am forever indebted to the makers of baby wipes. The ups included my famous scrambled eggs, cheese, sausage, and tobasco sauce rolled in a heated tortilla shell, a piece of key lime pie, and a very enjoyable two hour nap.

The highlight of the day would of course be the race from California, where Tony "2005 Nextel Cup Champion" Stewart enjoyed another stellar race, finishing 3rd. A rather uneventful race, of course until the caution with about 20 laps left, where everyone and their brother tried two tires, only to feel the heat as Riggs and Wimmer found the outside wall for a green/white checker ending. Kyle Busch held on and his two tire "mistake" gave him his first Nextel Cup Win, which also made him the youngest ever driver to win a Cup Race. It also saw Jeff Gordon drop from the 10th spot, with one race to go to make the "Chase". In Jeff's words, "We just suck!". Dad—I told you he wasn't going to make it in and I can just picture you handing me over our bet—a crisp $1 bill—after next Saturday night. (As earlier mentioned, I'll bet on anything with a wager involved!!). Ryan Newman is only 1 point out in 11th and I'm sure he is still the biggest fan that Dale Jarrett has.

Hope everyone has a great Labor Day and enjoys a good ole fashioned cookout. Thanks to Todd and Sara, I have pre-cooked brats in the freezer, so I'm all set!!

Ciao.

MONDAY, SEPTEMBER 05, 2005 10:48 PM, CDT
DAY 13—TRANSFUSIONS, TRANSFUSIONS, TRANSFUSIONS

I was sitting here thinking of a way to start this journal, when the idea came to me that if I had $5 for every transfusion I have ever had the past 3 1/2 years, I just might be able to pay cash for the 2005 Monte Carlo SS "Tony Stewart" Edition Car, that I keep telling my father I would like to own, but it seems my pleas have fallen upon death ears. The reason I bring this up, as I'm sure you're smart enough to figure out via the title of the journal entry, is because my transfusions finally began today.

I'll start out by saying that I was at the hospital today for 7 1/2 hours, three of which were spent in the conference room, before they were nice enough to provide me with a room with a TV, a comfortable chair, and a bed. I needed a platelet transfusion and a magnesium transfusion. The platelets I am used to. They fly into me in about 15 minutes. However, Madison was insistent on running them in over an hour today and seen as I didn't feel like arguing because I was stuck anyway, I let that happen, but not before I struck my own deal!!

Originally, they wanted to infuse platelets over an hour and magnesium over eight hours. Eight hours of transfusions, after I have already been there two hours, was not going to happen. I advised them of my platelet history and struck up the deal that they could transfuse them over an hour, if they cut my magnesium time and increased the dosage of my pills instead. Done Deal!! I had to sit there anyway for three hours to let the magnesium drip in, so why not let the platelets drip in at the same time for an hour!! No Brainer!!

The time at the hospital was spent trying to kill seven and a half hours and that was tough to do, but I managed. I then came home and took a nice long nap. Woke up, took care of some business, and am presently watching the Miami / FSU game, which is almost as terrible as Syracuse / West Virginia. 10-7 Miami. Just a fundamentally poor offensive and special team game. If you can't tell, defensive battles aren't my cup of tea in football. In hockey and baseball its just beautiful, but in football, talk about wasting three hours that I'll never get back.

Anyway—forgot to mention that wbc count down to 100, AST/ALT (liver enzyme) levels rising, Tacrolimus level stable at 5, and the rest you have been privy too. I meet with Dr. Juckett tomorrow after labs, so hoping he says we are still on track.

I hope everyone enjoys going back to work tomorrow. Someone needs to!! HA!!

TUESDAY, SEPTEMBER 06, 2005 11:50 PM, CDT
DAY 14—ONE WEEK ANNIVERSARY

It is with sweet pleasure that today I celebrate my bone marrow transplant one week anniversary!! How many people get to say that for the rest of their lives??!! I do and damn proud of it. Kick Ass and Rock On.

I did however, spend another 8 hours at the hospital, receiving platelets and magnesium. That kind of sucked, but a small price I have to pay and put up with. I will say though, that you would think I would do something productive in the eight hours, but how can someone be productive in the hospital? Instead I just killed time preparing for my fantasy football draft, made neat little charts to see who people were taking, ranked every player where I thought they should be, and low and behold, it was time to go home!! Unreal how time flies when you're having fun—right, right.

Rest of blood work was as normal—low wbc's, low hemoglobin, liver enzyme levels went down a bit and tacro up to 6 (again this needs to be between 5-15). Realistically, nothing short of what to expect after going through chemo. I met with Dr. Juckett today or I should say he came to where I was, and he was very pleased with the results so far. His facial expressions showed he was a bit surprised that things were going this well and seeing that helps keep me upbeat and positive. We did however go over what to expect in the next few weeks and I'm still knee deep in the woods, but it seems the fall is bringing down the leaves just enough to almost point my lost soul in the right direction. The only thing I don't like, is I have never been very good with directions before, so I'll have to work on that!! I confirmed that my blood type will switch from B+ to O. He said I will notice this when I start to turn jaundice and start to urinate what appears to be Coca-Cola. You couldn't believe my excitement when he said that—and I thought urinating green from VP16 (chemo) was kewl. Don't worry though, as I will take pictures—its all about simple pleasures and taking pride in weird experiences!! But—he hopes that it will be a gradual change and not a sudden change. It could happen anytime, so I'm keeping my eyes peeled!! If it is sudden, I will more than likely be hospitalized, as it could turn into a problem, so hoping for gradual. This will be totally different from the GVHD, which will occur later. More on that when and if it happens!!

So that has been my day—spent most of the day at the hospital, came home and crashed for three hours, and woke up to the Fantasy Football Draft, which Todd runs and Dad, Mark, Todd, and I are all apart of. I have no doubt I have a championship team and looking forward to putting the smack down on Dad when we face off here in Week 1!! Won't bore you with the rest of what happened during the draft.

As for taking care of some business:

1. Todd I will take your bet. For everyone, it is Todd's 1st and 24th pick (L. Tomlinson and K. Jones for Todd) vs. my 9th and 16th picks (Corey Dillon and Rudi Johnson). Should be a good battle and I think winner should have the choice of where they would like to go.

2. Kari Mattonen I will take your bet that you do not finish above Relli Racing 2 (which is my Dad's and my combined team). I will also bet you that I finish above you and take over from my bottom feeder position of 112th. Name the stakes and we got a rumble.

3. Congrats to Jodi Kleibel (Speaker before myself at benefit, mentor, and liver transplant recipient) who returned to work after two years post transplant. I tip my hat to you and am honored to follow in your footsteps. Chris—sure you are proud as hell!!

4. Congrats to my friends Lucky and Nikki who got engaged this past weekend and are enjoying their time in the UP, hey. (Thanks for filling me in Jenny and Mike. Mike—glad to hear your apnea is being controlled—bet you look cute in your nose mask!!).

5. To Amy—good luck in your first day of classes tomorrow.

6. To my cousins Tyler and Holly—Holly: I'm glad you weren't at my benefit, as I heard you had an awesome weekend playing hockey. Always choose to play the game—that is the best honor. Tyler: Thanks again for the Packer tickets, as Amy and her mom had a great time!!

7. To those who have e-mailed me—I'm slow at getting back right now, but you're on my list of things to do.

8. To my family—thanks for supporting my decision to go through with this transplant. One week and counting …

As Dr. Juckett said today, "Cheers".

WEDNESDAY, SEPTEMBER 07, 2005 11:10 PM, CDT
DAY 15—KEY LIME PIE

Today could possibly have been the most boring day out of the past two weeks. The hospital is starting to become as thrilling as an old joke. I have however hit rock bottom with my blood counts and my protective bubble has added a second coating.

My wbc's were at 100 (which means I have no immune system whatever and a fever means I'm stuck back in my "cell"). Needed platelets and magnesium again, so that killed another 7 hours of my day—new time record today though, so again simple pleasures to pass the day. Hemoglobin at 8.3 and will probably need blood transfusion tomorrow. Trying for the trifecta. Liver enzymes holding. I did make more of my time today, as I finished my Robert Ludlum book, finished my Esquire magazine, and even watched "Friday Night Lights", which I think is a dope movie. As for tomorrow, I plan to begin a new book called "The Bounty: The True Story of the Mutiny on the Bounty". If you have no clue what I am reading, I'm sure your history grade wasn't an A!!

I am growing ever tired and am having trouble catching my breath at times, due to my low blood counts. I did my laundry downstairs today and had to walk up and down two sets of stairs three times (wash, change, dry) and even though that took place over 2 hours time, it felt like I just took part in hockey suicides. So—I took close to a four hour nap, got up, watched a James Bond movie on TV for a bit, and rewarded my hard work for the day with a piece of Key Lime Pie. Key Lime Pie can turn the worst day into the best one!! Gotta love pleasures like that!!

THURSDAY, SEPTEMBER 08, 2005 10:46 PM, CDT
DAY 16—THE TRIFECTA

Two summers ago, Amy and I made a trip to Minnesota for the Basilica Block Fest and to hang out for a weekend. Well on that Saturday, we took a trip to Canterbury Park for the dog races. Now beforehand, we were eating lunch with Todd and Sara, Dad, and Grandma. We had a plan to pick 3 numbers and place a $2 bet on each race (there were 10 races) with the numbers we chose. Dad and Todd ended up throwing in $20 each and picker there own three numbers and off Amy and I went to the track.

Well its funny that this has come up because yesterday in my journal I had written that today I was going for the transfusion trifecta. I was simply being funny and I've always ridden a fine line on getting what you wish for. Two years ago, Amy and I hit a trifecta that paid around $200 with our numbers for the day. (We thought we hit a second one, but replay showed our 3 dog finished just behind the actual 3 dog). Of course that meant $50 for everyone involved in the fiasco and a good laugh was had by all.

Today I hit the trifecta at the hospital and I can tell you I did not laugh. Today I received platelets, two units of blood, and 6 grams of magnesium. Funny story—in Appleton, platelets go in over 15 minutes and blood goes in at a max of 200ml per hour or roughly 5 hours. In Madison, platelets go in over an hour (I have not defended my 15 minute streak in Appleton because I am stuck anyway), but was surprised that they run blood in at 300ml per unit. That's flipping fast. I have to sweet talk my way into 200ml in Apple. they ask me if 300ml per hour is okay here. HA!! Either way, timing didn't matter much as the magnesium had to drip in over four and a half hours anyway. Today I set a new time record going to and from the hospital in just under 9 hours. I was not thrilled to have hit the "trifecta" as it didn't pay out a damn thing. Then I thought about it and every time I get blood or platelets, someone is saving my life. Otherwise, I would run out and we know the end result of that. So—three people saved my life today and magnesium keeps me from a host of problems: I recommend checking out:

http://www.mbschachter.com/importance_of_magnesium_to_human.htm

for more information on magnesium and nutrition. I offer this because this is a learning journal and as I learn, so will you!!

Anyway—back to trifectas. I woke up from my too short of nap too watch the NE/OAK game, which I have found to be the game I was missing all weekend—Moss is unreal and New England looks good!! But, I called Todd before the game to wish him "Happy Birthday (33rd)" and thought of how his ID was my ticket to some fond memories a few years back and I forgot he was in Indianapolis. Anyway—I asked him what he was doing and low and behold, he was in a limo bus on the way to the horse track to cash in on his piece of the "trifecta" today. Hoping a phone call tomorrow brings good news!!

But—that is all from here. As for some life advice, "Trifectas come in all shapes and sizes; they can be bet or experienced; you win or you lose; you decide the silver lining." And take some time to learn about the wonders of magnesium found at your local vitamin franchise.

FRIDAY, SEPTEMBER 09, 2005 10:32 PM, CDT
DAY 17—GOOD NEWS OR FALSE HOPE?

Today I ventured into the unknown grounds of the UW-Madison cafeteria and tried a main dish from the kitchen. It was roast pork loin and mashed potatoes, along with Cocoa Krispies as a backup. I was presently surprised and can now honestly say that I have had a decent meal from a hospital cafeteria. Those Cocoa Krispies were phenomenal!! Seriously though, the pork was not as good as being marinated in apple juice for the night and slowly roasted on the grill, but it wasn't bad and I would have it again—never thought I would say that in a cafeteria!!

Today's length of stay turned out to be just like any other day, the only difference being I only received magnesium, 6 grams of magnesium at that!! The attempt today was to give me enough today so that I wouldn't need any tomorrow and could enjoy the weekend. My wbc also went up to a whopping total of 200, my platelets held above 20, and my blood held about 8.0. So as I mentioned earlier, "Good news or false hope".

Tomorrow is a rather monumental day as well, as I test my above mentioned statement and I also receive my fourth and final injection of methotrexate. In two weeks or so, we will see if the methotrexate and tacrolimus (which they increased to 3 pills twice a day or a total of 6mg per day) have been useful in protecting against the GVHD.

Besides that, boring and uneventful; just how we like it right now. Boring and uneventful.

SATURDAY, SEPTEMBER 10, 2005 11:34 PM, CDT
DAY 18—GOOD NEWS OR FALSE HOPES PART II

Today was full of minor achievements, no real setbacks, but a case of some things I thought was over.

Amy and I started off to the hospital this morning and as we checked in to the 6th floor, we were told the methotrexate would be ready at 9 a.m. and we would be taken care of soon. We were put into a room and forgot about for awhile. Finally at 9 a.m., Janice came in and drew labs and said she would be back with the methotrexate. At 9:45, Amy and I were tired of waiting as we wanted some breakfast, so we left for the cafeteria. We were so thrilled when we arrived and saw two plates of french toast under the "red lights" and a hash brown, egg, and something else plate adjoining it. That was all that was left for breakfast, as it closed at 9:30 a.m.. Now disappointed and still hungry, Amy decided to have a pumpkin nut bread slice and I protested against the cafeteria and purchased nothing.

Anyway—got back up into the room and continued to play the waiting game. Janice came back in around 10:30 and said that the labs were all finally back and that my wbc held at 200, platelets held at 25,000, hemoglobin at 9.9, liver enzymes a bit higher but stable, my tacrolimus level had risen to 8 (yesterdays result), but I still needed magnesium. So as you can imagine, I had to wait around for the magnesium and still had not had my methotrexate. Close to 11:00 a.m., Amy and I decided to try our hand at lunch. But as we were about to leave, I suddenly fell ill and couldn't even make it to the bathroom to throw-up and the sink took the fury. After a brief pause, I rushed into the bathroom to continue. I haven't been nauseous for almost a week, so I popped a lorazepam, gathered myself, and we went for lunch.

My protest against the cafeteria ended and a I took pleasure in a brat and bag of chips, while Amy made a salad. We came back up to the room and low and behold, my magnesium and methotrexate were waiting for me!! Janice came in shortly after we got back and hung the magnesium and prepared the methotrexate. She asked if I wanted a popsicle. I looked at her as if she were crazy and just laughed. I asked her if she asked me if I wanted a popsicle and yes I heard her right. I laughed again. She said she was serious, as people that get methotrexate experience throat irritation during injection and often suck on a popsicle to get past that. Well one, I was never offered a popsicle the other three times, two I now felt like a jackass for laughing at her, so three, I politely declined. A popsicle—how funny. Anyway—everything went well and we were out of the hospital around 1 p.m.—shortest day in a long time!! Here is where "Good News or False Hope" begins part II: the methotrexate is supposed to lower the counts for a day or two before they recover. If that is the case, as I hadn't paid much attention the other times as I knew I was going to crash anyway, it could make for a long day tomorrow and/or slow my recovery. In a few hours we will know!!

After the hospital, Amy and I made a run to the bank and the grocery store, which would become my first interaction with non-hospitalized humans, in quite some time. We decided to try it out cause it wouldn't be busy with the Badgers being on and I would rest my fate with my mask. Off we went to Copps, which had a bank inside of it, and were in and out within a half hour. We then ventured to a video store for a few movies and all was clear!!! Minor achievement accomplished—end result to be determined later!!

I took a nice long nap when I got home and have just finished watching the NASCAR Race, as the "Chase for the Cup" is now set. I immediately called my Dad after the race and demanded payment for our $1 bet as Jeff Gordon missed the race. I off course was laughed at, but am full of pride for winning the bet!! Rather boring race, but I'm sure Tony Raines will get what is coming to him. Congrats to Notre Dame for beating Michigan at home—maybe now Ann Arbors yappers will zip it and Congrats to THE University of Texas for defeating THE Ohio State University and now maybe people from Columbus will stop referring to Ohio State University as THE Ohio State University because they now look no better than the Alamo Game Lock. I didn't know Iowa State even had a football team—I guess Iowa found out they did. How the mighty have fallen and so many doors were opened today and so many were damn near destroyed—gotta love it!! Funny how I have had the pleasure of being at everyone of those places at some point in my past—small world it is.

Anyway—my head has been a bit off today, which means my balance has too, so I'm going to bed early on this young Saturday Night. Until after the NFL tomorrow—Ciao.

SUNDAY, SEPTEMBER 11, 2005 10:28 PM, CDT
DAY 19—A QUICK DAY

The 11th of September brings back many different emotions for me. That date seems to be born of many great memories that have not yet faded and can be seen clear as day. It was roughly about 13 hours earlier today eastern time, that I happened to be at the Pentagon Metro Station, which is under the Pentagon itself, when the "plane" hit. I remember rushing out of the station with thousands of people fleeing the Pentagon itself and the metro stations. When we all finally made it up the stairs, we were greeted with a first hand view of "whatever" had just happened—and was just awestruck. Being who I am, I tried to run closer to the area to help out, but was about halfway there when I was met by some armed uniformed officials who advised me to turn around and follow the rest of the people to a safety area. Many other interesting stories about that day and it was weird to see the most powerful city in America, turn into a sullen city to walk around the next few weeks. Anyway—there is interesting new video out (Discovery) has been showing and the camera's placed on the outside walls of the Pentagon show no airplane hitting the wall—just an immense streak of light. Now I'm not saying anything indifferent, but if you look at the photos of 9/11 at the Pentagon, there is no plane debris. That's a pretty big plane to disappear immediately and the heat wouldn't disintegrate a plane that quick and the wings probably would have fallen off to the side. I off course am no expert nor can I figure out how you make that many people disappear that were on that flight. Plus there is not one video of a plane flying into the Pentagon, but clear videos in New York. Also interesting how a plane goes down in the middle of Pennsylvania that had a course set for D.C. I also keep forgetting my roommate in D.C. was in the Army, cleaned up the debris at the Pentagon, and answered all my questions as "no comment" or "classified". I offer this website just for something to get the creative parts of the American taxpayer going:

http://www.pentagonstrike.co.uk/

There are other sites also, but I'll start everyone slow.

Anyway, seen as we are not here for Matt's interesting theories on government abatement, I'll get back to the fact that today was not a record, but Amy and I were only at the hospital for 5 1/2 hours. Needed magnesium, blood and platelets held from the methotrexate yesterday, wbc's the same at 300, and tacro level at 8. Tomorrow should be a good indication if things are coming up or just stabilizing, so looking forward to finding out.

Anyway—its been a quick day. Laid down this afternoon about 3:30ish and woke up at 9:00 p.m. and ready to go back to bed. Didn't watch too much football today, so I guess my comments will have to suffice as "Kramer—I'm liking our bet". I bet Kramer before the regular season that the Pack wouldn't win more than 7 games. At least everyone else in the division lost too, as Detroit will surely find a way to blow it, along with a few receivers.

So—on an Anniversary I'm fond of and not so fond off, I will bid goodnight and a good work week to those attending!!

MONDAY, SEPTEMBER 12, 2005 11:24 PM, CDT
DAY 20—JUST ANOTHER DAY

Sometimes I feel like I am living the lyrics of a song and today would have to be "Just Another Day". I made my way to the hospital on a semi-new shortcut in order to avoid the school traffic and it worked fairly smooth. I arrived at the hospital at 8:30, just like every day. Then I purchased a coffee from the Java Coffee Bar and the counter lady (whose name I can't remember at this moment) said I was right on time. "Sure am—how are you, etc, etc, have a good day!!". Then off to check in and chat with the receptionists at the cancer clinic for a minute, then off to check in at the chemotherapy infusion area, where they say "HI—Come on Back" all in one breath. The jokingly tell me to find my own was to Bay 28—the same Bay I have every day—and that my nurse will be in shortly.

Stefani comes in to take my vitals and we chat about the weekend and how her wedding in Chicago was. Then Jodi comes in and asks the same questions they ask everyday—I tell her to copy and paste, but then she reminds me its Monday and they need a new sheet for the week—okay ... the blood lab comes to take my blood from me and then 10:30 a.m. comes. 10:30 a.m. is important, as this is my lunch time. I have enough time to walk down to the cafeteria and back up, in order to catch the start of "Who's making my dinner?". Now this is a really stupid show, but two cooks face off with a certain set of ingredients and have to make 3 or 4 dinner options for the featured guest in 20 minutes. They they have a 10 minute desert bake off, where they come up with 2 or 3 deserts. A winner is declared and that's it. Exciting hey!!

Anyway—10:30 a.m. is lunch, 11:00 a.m. is this baking show, and 12:00 p.m. is Days. Somewhere between 10:30 a.m. and 11:30 a.m.

(most days) lab results come in. Today they came in around 12:00 p.m. and I needed magnesium, wbc raised to 400, platelets holding at 21,000, hemo at 9.9, and liver enzymes alright. They have decreased my tacrolimus down to 2mgs, twice a day, down from the 3mgs, twice a day. But—they hung the 6 grams of magnesium at 12:25 p.m. and it would run over the next four hours.

I spent the afternoon reading and dozing off and after my over 8 hour stint, was allowed to go home. I came home and crashed and woke up just in time for Monday Night Football. Now its time to go back to bed and get ready for tomorrow.

Today was just another day. Just like the song—just another day. That's all I have—just like any other day. As Jeff Gordon said on Saturday Night, "We're done—we're done now". HA!

TUESDAY, SEPTEMBER 13, 2005 11:45 PM, CDT
DAY 21—I LOVE VACATION DAYS

Have you ever been in a situation where you didn't quite know how to react because it would either give you away for what you were attempting or you end up laughing so hard because you just pulled off something that you never thought you could?? That happened to my brother Todd and I today and I'll keep you in suspense until later so you have to read the whole journal entry and just because I can. I love the question Why?—"Because I can". So innocent, yet when tactfully used, charming!! Haha.

Today started a bit quicker than yesterday as I made a quick run through my daily chats and was back in Bay 28 in no time. The lab was in to take my labs in a few minutes and Cindy had my vitals done soon after. Today the copy and paste was back in effect, so 100 questions was avoided—love those days. Well it came to be 9:30 a.m. and I already had nothing to do as I had to kill the time from 10:00 a.m. to 11:00 a.m. by reading the paper before my chef show came on. So—I went to eat breakfast, which is out of my routine, but anyway—I decided on oatmeal, which was in a dish with a cover on it, and got another cup full of brown sugar, and then decided on Apple Jacks for a backup. When I returned to my room, I opened up my oatmeal and found out it was actually grits. Now I don't know how everyone else feels, but oatmeal and grits are not the same and I don't like grits. Apple Jacks it was!!

I was talking to my brother Todd who was coming into town for a quick visit and some business, when my labs came in. I'll give everyone a guess what I needed today and you would all be right. But, there was something alarming about my tacrolimus level from yesterday and also as today's came back. My tacrolimus level has risen to 18 as of today and that is not good for me—effects can be very serious and it could easily explain my balance issues the last two days and why it takes me so long to focus on certain things—sometimes I feel like I'm in the "Butterfly Effect", just before he passes through—if you've seen it, then you know what I'm talking about.

Todd showed up a bit after noon and we went down to the cafeteria for some food and ended up running into Paul Westphal, whose son Corey was down for a 4 hour drip which he seems to have weekly, and we chatted for a bit. It sounds as if Corey is doing well and that's awesome—keep it up Corey. The cafeteria is quite busy at lunch time and I was miserable around all those people and knew why I always come down before the storm. Todd made his salad and back up we went.

Dr. Juckett came in shortly after we were back in "my bay" and he asked some questions, told him some of the feelings I have been experiencing, and he checked me out. We talked about my levels and how everything is good except the magnesium and tacrolimus. He took me off of the tacrolimus for the next two doses (tonight and tomorrow morning) because we need to lower that level quick. The magnesium has everyone a bit puzzled, as they are infusing me and I'm taking 2000mg a day. Dr. Juckett asked how I was handling that and I told him I was actually a bit blocked up—he just raised his eyes and said, "that's interesting as patients I have on that much can't get off the toilet"!!! My checkup in all went fine and then he said that he was going to give me the day off tomorrow from coming in. I'm not quite sure why, but I love vacation days and quickly agreed with his decision. (The more I am thinking about it, the more I am wondering what I am going to do—still can't go out anywhere without my mask, so I'll probably sleep in until the "cooking show" and "Days", then take a nap, and then have a quiet evening!!).

(My entry is over 5000 characters so it is being split here—sorry for the delay and wordy document).

TUESDAY, SEPTEMBER 13, 2005 11:46 PM, CDT
DAY 21—I LOVE VACATIONS DAYS CONT ...

Now to the continuation of my story to start today: Todd and I were allowed to leave the hospital around 2:00ish and went to Copps because I had a coupon for a 24 pack of Dasani water for $3.59. That's a good deal and I wanted to cash in on it. We made our way to the water isle and they were all out of the cases of water and it clearly stated on the coupon "while supplies last". I've always been one to try things anyway, so I started to grab some 6 packs of Dasani water and Todd asked what I was doing. I handed him two six packs, I picked up two sick packs, and we went to check out. Now I picked out an older cashier and as we put the water down and she started scanning, I gave her the coupon and said, "You are all out of cases, so I just picked up four 6 packs". She was already confused and then rang all four 6 packs through. The total was like $10.50 cause they were $2.50 a piece. She then managed to take off $3.59 and I told her that the coupon was for 24 bottles for $3.59 and not just $3.59 off. At this point, I thought Todd and I were done. Todd was laughing and I was able to hide behind my mask. Well, then she took off another $3.59 or something like that and now the total for the water was $2.98, which was $0.61 cheaper than the coupon. She tried to ring it as a sale and it wouldn't go through. Now Todd and I are literally rolling at this point and she called over the manager to give her a price override so she could finish checking us out. The manager came over, took a look around, and then just overrode the price. So I handed the clerk a $5 bill and she gave me $2.02 back—fiddled with coupon—and Todd and I walked out as quickly as we could. Once outside, we couldn't hold it in any longer and surely looked guilty of some evil scheme to any passer by. I loaded the water into my trunk and off we went. Lesson learned—you never know until you try!!

\But—I am happy to say and it should be no surprise, that my two week anniversary was celebrated at home with Todd, as I introduced him to the show "House" on Fox, which I think is just hilarious. We had Pizza Pit pizza and I ended with nothing else but a piece of key lime pie!!

I am looking forward to my day of sleeping in tomorrow and having the day off. Nothing like a day off—well there is, but we all know what that is, so no need to elaborate—funny that I have a day off from having the day off. Would make a good analytical puzzle rhyme if worded correctly—well I'm just full of good ideas today!! Off to finish "The Mutiny" … goodnight.

WEDNESDAY, SEPTEMBER 14, 2005 11:15 PM, CDT
DAY 22—CULVERS ROCKS

Today can really be summed as a "resting day off". I slept in until a bit after 10:00 a.m. and then my brother Todd came over in between business meetings. We decided to go to Culvers to lunch and low and behold, the "Flavor of the Day" was Key Lime Pie!!! I can say from a few hours ago, that is was mighty tasty. Over lunch, I introduced Todd to my "Make My Dinner" show and he had a few laughs.

The rest of the day was not filled with too much excitement. Played around on the computer to find some new music, took care of some bills, and took care of some miscommunications between insurance carriers and the misc. hospitals I have visited. In general a frustrating experience until you talk to the right person. Then it was off for an afternoon rest.

When I woke up this morning, I noticed that my hair has started to fall out. So rather than wake up tomorrow with it all over my pillow, I shaved it off and cleaned my look up a bit—now I look like your typical chemo patient with no hair, a mask on, and making my way to the hospital!!!

This evening I did more searching for some music and am now ready for bed. What a long and frustrating day spent on the computer, the phone, and in bed. Definitely a break in my routine—Ha. Just have to keep telling myself that nothing is boring and boring is good!!

THURSDAY, SEPTEMBER 15, 2005 11:30 PM, CDT
DAY 23—FAIRIES AND GOLD

Have you ever been so transposed on something that your brain sensors are working every emotion at one time and you are thinking about something, while watching something, and writing something, and yet you are doing all of them at the same time without missing a beat, a thought, or a word? Kind of like being in the zone, but a bit more complicated.

That's how I've felt the last 2 hours as I was watching the movie "Crash" that was just released as a rental. That movie just blew my mind away. Brilliant. Absolutely brilliant. Very strong, emotional, passionate, and thought provoking. I would recommend it be on the top of your rental list. If you have seen it or when you see it, you should realize what my journal title means—if not, you must summon the power to use both sides of your brain and not just the left or right!!

In all reality, today has been a very good day and I have achieved a goal I didn't have any control over, except that I made it with myself to keep me motivated and something to look forward to. As most of you know from previous journals, that the band "Lucero" is my new favorite and as I acquire all the previous albums, I realize more and more why. Wish I could have discovered them a few years ago and I could have been like all the "Dead Heads", but been a "Lucero Head" for a bit!! Anyway (I need a better transition word than that, as I use it more than one should), before I came to the hospital for the transplant, I knew that they were going to be playing in Chicago on Sept. 23rd. I told myself that I would be at that concert, even if I was in a protective bubble. I am happy to say that I won't need to be in a protective bubble and I will be in attendance. I wish it were next Friday right now!! (They are playing with a new band named "Limbeck" and Keith—you should check them out too—also check out "Beverly" as they are new in California—you can check them both out on MySpace.com). There is no better feeling than setting a goal and realizing it—waiting until Friday to truly celebrate, but back to the reason why ...

I met with Dr. Juckett again today and my labs are ever recovering nicely. Hemo rising, platelets rising, and white count rising. I now have 600 wbc, with 150 neutrophils. Making neutrophils means that I am less susceptible to serious infections!! I still need to be careful, but in a weeks time, I should be in smooth sailing as far as my counts. My tacro level has fallen from 18 to 7 in the past two days, so again we have that under control!! My magnesium was once again low, but they have decided to not transfuse any. They are trying to see if my levels stay stable without any, if I am wasting it, or if the transfusions are doing anything. So in essence, I do not have to go back to the hospital until MONDAY—YEP—MONDAY. How awesome is that??!! Monday will be a big day as it should shed some light on the mag. level and will be a test on the tacro level to see if its going to stay!!

I celebrated today's events with my famous homemade pizza, recipe courtesy of dad. Then I just had to top it off with a piece of key lime pie (imagine that) and here I am—I've made it out of the hospital, my counts are stabilizing, I get to go see Lucero, and all before Day 30 post transplant, where the most threatening battle starts. I'm sure I'll have the rejuvenation I need from the Lucero concert, that I'll make a vow to see another one!!!

Fairies and Gold. Fairies and Gold.

PS: Tracey—thanks for the post. I have the album already as I like stupid country music too. I had hoped they had a story behind it, but found out someone just wrote it and it has no personal meaning to them. Still reminds me of me though!!

FRIDAY, SEPTEMBER 16, 2005 10:47 PM, CDT
DAY 24—SHORT DAY

I woke at just before noon today—guess that's what happens when you have the day off and when you don't fall asleep until 2 a.m., either cause I just couldn't sleep or my book kept my interest for that long. Regardless, I took an afternoon nap around 5:00 p.m. to 7:00 p.m.-ish and not here it is just a tad past 10:00 p.m. and I'm ready to crash.

Reading the above, you can tell its been a tough day and I accomplished a whole lot. I did however take a drive to visit "University Ridge Golf Course" which I expect to be playing sometime soon here. Gorgeous. I also made my way to State Street to see where it was, as its the first time I have been that way since I have been down here. Found a route there and a new one home—liking knowing I can get around a bit!!

I received a phone call from a friend from college that I haven't talked to in a few years and even though it was long overdue, still made my day.

That's it—nothing exciting, no stories, behaving myself, and a night or two from finishing "The Real Story of the Mutiny on the Bounty" if anyone is interested!!

PS—watch out for my Tennessee Vols rolling into Florida tomorrow night to hand Urban Meyer a true taste of the SEC at Florida after Spurrier.

SATURDAY, SEPTEMBER 17, 2005 11:28 PM, CDT
DAY 25—YEAH, YEAH, YEAH

Yeah, Yeah, Yeah—three words that would seem to give a positive vibe and meaning, however when combined as one word used as a phrase, translates into nothing less than frustration and disappointment and having to eat your words. I'll explain.

In this Thursdays issue of the "Isthmus"—local Madison paper with the weeks events and city happenings—advertised were two things that caught my eye. One was an annual book sale on Monroe Street and the other was concert tickets that went on sale for Dierks Bentley and Cross Canadian Ragweed at the Orpheum. CCR rocks and I was planning on getting tickets right away at 10:00 a.m., but the book sale was at 10:00 a.m. In essence, I just forgot to get the tickets and so I just tried a few minutes ago and after looking at Ticketmaster and the CCR website, CCR is no longer holding that date and will not be playing in Madison. Glad I didn't get the tickets, disappointed they aren't coming. "Yeah, Yeah, Yeah". I did however make it to the book sale at 10:00 a.m., which turned out to be like 5 shelves of stuff and a few tables and no room to look, as it was take a number and wait your turn to look at the shelves—I was all excited for the book sale and "Yeah, Yeah, Yeah"—good thing I was there right away.

As I returned home, I figured I would do my laundry and get ready for a day of football. I gathered my laundry and dragged it downstairs, only to find someone filling the last two washers available. Off course I should have checked beforehand, but those stairs are a killer. So now I walked back upstairs with my laundry and had to sit for a few minutes. Three hours later I decided to try again, only this time going down to the laundry room first to see if there were any open washers. There were two, which was absolutely perfect. I walked back upstairs, got my laundry, and walked down. This time, there was a guy throwing laundry into the two open machines and I was like how in the span of two minutes does that happen?? "Yeah, Yeah, Yeah"—I can see where this is going—my laundry is sitting in the hallway, I'm pissed at it, and I figure I have plenty of clothes for at least 3 or 4 more days.

During this whole fiasco, I had the pleasure of watching the ND/MSU game—great first half—I figured I could nap for about 45 minutes and then wake up to watch the end. At 7:30 p.m. I had to look up the score on the internet to see I missed MSU winning in overtime. "Yeah, Yeah, Yeah". On top of that, the Tennessee game was already on, so my disappointment improved as my Vols were going to crush Florida in the "Swamp". I don't want to hear anything—"Yeah, Yeah, Yeah" and all that hoorah. If Fulmer would stick to one damn quarterback and give the offense some room to open it up, they would be 2-0. Instead Florida remains undefeated and I'm left with a full year to steam over the loss.

So now you are all familiar with a "Yeah, Yeah, Yeah" day. Maybe tomorrow it will be a "Yeah, Yeah, Yeah" day with the antonym playing its verses. I have a feeling it may just be, as "The Chase" begins tomorrow and Tony Stewart is on the pole, 5 points ahead, and soon to be 10 points ahead of everyone after lap 1!!!! Let's go Racing!! (Oh yeah—the Packers play too)!!

SUNDAY, SEPTEMBER 18, 2005 10:54 PM, CDT
DAY 26—SHERMAN'S A JOKE

You are now having a chance to play Head Coach of the Green Bay Packers for a play. Just one play—what do you do. Here is the situation: You are down by 12. You need two touchdowns to win the game. There is 9 minutes left. Your defense sucks and your offense has finally shown some life. You get screwed on an interference no call on 3rd down, its 4th down, and you are on the opponents 25 yard line. Do you: 1. Punt it. 2. Run a draw play because the defense is expecting pass. 3. Go for it—you need two touchdowns and one right here would be great. (Heck Charlie did it on 4th and 13 on the opponents 40 yard line and he was already down 7 points and it was 6 minutes into the game). If you don't make it, you have the opponent at their own 25 and still need two scores. 4. Kick a worthless field goal that makes it a 9 point play, still need two scores, and then kick off and let them run to the 40 yard line. In this choice, you also know your defense couldn't stop a pee wee league team with a wide receiver and a burner on the outside. If you picked any choice other than 4, you are smarter than a head coach in the NFL. If you picked 4, I would like to visit your planet for a few minutes. Nuff Said.

Congrats to Tony Stewart for finishing 2nd in the first of 10 races for the "Chase for the Cup". Newman may now be a force—first win this year. Robby Gordon should never be allowed on a NASCAR track again, but nice helmet toss. Did enjoy his quote on live TV and did enjoy the spectacle, but way to close to involving Stewart and that might not have settled so well. Either way—Robby Gordon and Mike Sherman should get together and talk strategy—what a "think tank" that would be.

For those of you wondering—best time to do laundry is during the Packer Game—wide open!!

That's my day—return to the hospital tomorrow for an important check up and see where I stand after the weekend. Routing for stable Tacro level and Magnesium counts, with rising counts on the blood. Break!!

MONDAY, SEPTEMBER 19, 2005 11:10 PM, CDT
DAY 27—COUNTS ARE GOOD!!

I was back in familiar territory today—among the present regulars at the Chemotherapy Bay, in my always open Bay 29, with Stephanie taking my vitals and Erica drawing my blood. The only difference from previous visits, was the my mother was with me, as she came into town late yesterday.

The Counts came back rather quick today and everything is looking good. Hemoglobin and Platelets still rising slowly, wbc was at 1500 with 865 neutrophils (had 150 on last Thursday), so my fear of infection has greatly reduced and just a few more neutrophils from being neutropenic. My magnesium was at 1.4, which is still low. However, it was at 1.3 on Thursday, so the good news is that it is holding itself by just taking 2000mg a day, and it seems the transfusions have just been wasted, which kind of seems in hindsight like a waste of time, but its always better to error on the side of hindsight, as is the plan!! Counts are good and that is important was we start to reach Day 30 here.

I spent the afternoon watching "A Very Long Engagement" which was a good flick. It's a foreign film in French, so its tough to watch and read at the same time, but at least I learned a bit of French today. Its kind of a chick flick, but it's set in WWI, so I guess you could call it a foreign "Pearl Harbor". Then I had a productive 3 hour nap and woke up in time to watch the premiere of "Surface"—not sure on it yet—probably end up like "Lost" where its good for a few weeks, you get tired of it, and then catch up to see the end.

Glad to see another high scoring NFL game here on Monday night—they keep at this rate and one NHL team will outscore 10 or 12 teams combined. Ha. I think I might change careers after this stint is over and become a "Jim Rome", but actually have something worthwhile to say. Right Jim Everett!!

PS—At this time in four days, Lucero.

PSS—Where did Santana Moss and Mark Brunell come from in the past 10 minutes I have been writing this? The Over still doesn't have a prayer to cover!!

TUESDAY, SEPTEMBER 20, 2005 10:52 PM, CDT
DAY 28—THREE WEEKS

Three weeks post transplant and I can't believe its been that long already—guess that's what happens when you are only awake for 10 hours a day. Kind of just laughed at the thought that I am awake just as long as some people work in a M-F job week. Well even if you all aren't amused, at least I am!!

I am pretty wore out today as I missed my afternoon nap. The reason being, is that I didn't get up until noon and had some running around to do. Even though the apartment is fully furnished here, I can't stand the sheets. I have given them there full due time and know that I am more aware of my surroundings and things, I needed some "Matt Approved Sheets", which need to be Egyptian Cotton and a rather nice thread count. Now I couldn't afford what I really wanted, but did settle for a nice baby blue queen set of sheets—I know I sound terrible right there, but its just one of those things I've learned after spending so much time recuperating in beds!! At least it was cheaper than Kramer's new 42" Plasma TV, but at least now he can watch the NASCAR Race in HD—right Kramer!!

The rest of the day was spent just driving around seeing where things are around this city—basically something to do to get out of the apartment and feel like an integral part of society for a few hours. During those few hours, you'll never guess in a million years what I bought. I know what you all are thinking and you're close, but not right. I was at Woodman's getting a few groceries and I went down the soda aisle and noticed that Faygo (think the last time I had a Faygo it was after a Little League game) now makes Diet Faygo soda's. Now they have all your regular flavors of grape, orange, cola, etc, but one caught my eye. DIET KEY LIME PIE SODA. Not kidding ya. Did I buy one? Of course I did—a 20oz. bottle for $0.38. How was it—tasted like key lime pie. I'm savoring it—having a little here and a little there—but yeah—diet key lime pie soda. Still laughing.

Have a new band for everyone—"Bascom Hill". Worth a listen and then a purchase. They are local here in Madison, so if anyone listens to them (can be found on Myspace.com) and likes them,

Exclusive Company down here sells them, so I can send you out one for a small finders fee!!

Other than that—I am extremely psyched as twelve hours from right now, I will have finished Hole Number 1 at Odana Hills. I don't know if I have enough swings in me to finish 18 holes, but we're gonna find out!!! Kick Ass and bring on the energy drinks!!

Ciao.

WEDNESDAY, SEPTEMBER 21, 2005 11:40 PM, CDT
DAY 29—BINGO, BANGO, BONGO

Today was one heck of a day and all I did was one thing!! I woke up earlier than normal this morning, as I was meeting my friend Ben at Odana Hills here in Madison, so that we could play a round of golf. That's right—I finally made it outside for a morning and part of the afternoon and didn't have to worry about a thing cause there is never a crowd on a golf course—at least not watching me play!!

Seen as we only had a twosome—they paired us with Chi—he was golfing by himself and was walking the course—the kicker—he was 74 years old. I'm 28 and I couldn't think of walking two holes right now and here Chi was—heck of a player for being 74. He didn't talk a whole lot or say much to us and we couldn't really tell if he was enjoying playing with us cause Ben and I were joking around and playing Bingo, Bango , Bongo, which I will get back to but at the turn, Chi asked us if we were playing 18. We said, "yes" and he said okay. Then we parked the cart and we're going inside for to get something to drink—Chi says to us as we are going in, "I go play now". Ben and I said "Okay" and then we looked at each other and I said, "Is that a nice way of saying "I don't want to play with you two anymore"?". We had a good laugh anyway!!

But back to golfing—Ben and I ended up playing Bingo, Bango, Bongo, which is first on, closest to, and first in. Of course you have to gamble on the golf course, so we played a $1 a point. More on that later.

As for my actual golf—was very impressed with myself. I parred two par 5's, double bogeyed two 3 par 3's, and triple bogeyed one par 3!! That should have a few of you laughing hysterically right now. Needless to say, my putting wasn't on fire, although my two best shots were about 40 foot putts that I drained—how—its better to be lucky than good sometimes!! Anyway, when all was said and done, I shot a 98 and my goal for the day was to shoot under 100, so goal 2 set and accomplished. (Goal 1 was get out of hospital, Goal 2 was play round of golf under 100, and Goal 3 was to be in Chicago on Friday for "Lucero"—oh so close I can hear it). The bad news, was that my 98 didn't compare so well to Ben's 79, so needless to say, Bingo, Bango, Bongo came down to me having to buy lunch!!

I had a par on hole 18 to end the round and then Ben and I went to the "Great Dane Pub" to eat, which was not bad. Tried something new—yeah I was scared too—and had a Cuban Sandwich, which was spiced pork, ham, and swiss on a French roll pressed together. It wasn't bad—wasn't bad.

Spent the rest of the afternoon taking a nice four hour nap, got up just before "Lost", which continues to suck me in—I have all kinds of ideas if anyone really cares to chat about them—and I'll just leave you with the word "Lemuria" to search.

Anyway—one more step taken to normalcy—but why is the light so damn far away??

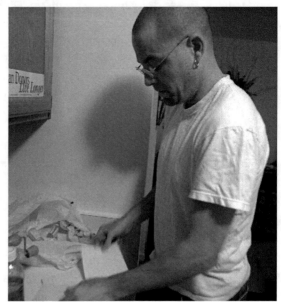

Matt Morrell writes down the amount left in each of his pill bottles before leaving Oshkosh for the hospital in Madison, WI.
Photo by Wm. Glasheen

Turning into the University of Wisconsin Madison hospital for a twice weekly visit.
Photo by Wm. Glasheen

Matt stops to smoke a cigarette before entering the clinic for his weekly tests and transfusions in Madison, WI. "I know I'm in a place where there's nothing that I can do to help the situation and having a cigarette is not going to make anything worse; it's not going to make anything better. So I'm going to go out on my terms. Even though I'm going through all this, I'm going to live my life to what I want during these last few months and that includes having a cigarette here and there."
January 26, 2006
Photo by Wm. Glasheen

Playing some of his favorite music using his computer as a stereo.
Photo by Wm. Glasheen

Amy Glasheen and Matt Morrell watch Matt's favorite channel, Discovery, on a quiet morning in their Oshkosh, WI, apartment. Leg and joint pain along with fatigue keep Matt close to home several days a week.
February 1, 2006
Photo by Wm. Glasheen

Matt celebrates a Duke victory over rival North Carolina with his friend and fellow Duke fan, Frank Revels, at a Greenville, WI, sports bar.
February 7, 2006
Photo by Wm. Glasheen

Matt and his girlfriend Amy leave the Oshkosh, WI, apartment that they share to drop Amy off at class, and to return a few rented videos.
Photo by Wm. Glasheen

Matthew Morrell
Photo by Wm. Glasheen

Matt and Amy ride the elevator to the parking garage of their Oshkosh, WI, apartment as Amy, a nursing student at U.W. Oshkosh, heads for class and Matt for a cup of coffee. Amy says she decided to become a nurse following Matt's bone marrow transplant.
February 1, 2006
Photo by Wm. Glasheen

Matt Morrell, 28, explains his health problems over coffee at a diner in Appleton, WI. Matthew was diagnosed with Type one diabetes and advanced cryptogenic liver cirrhosis due to autoimmune disease and in need of a transplant in 2001. Two years later with the liver problems being managed and his name on the transplant list, he was diagnosed with leukemia.
January 12, 2006
Photo for the Post Crescent by Wm. Glasheen

Matt shares a smile while joking with the staff at the welcome desk in the U.W.
Wisconsin Hospital's hematology clinic during his weekly visit.
January 26, 2006
Photo for the Post Crescent by Wm. Glasheen

Matt picks up a jar of moisturizing cream for his girlfriend Amy while wait-
ing for his prescriptions to be refilled. "Every time I go to the pharmacy
Amy always seems to run out of cream or lotion, so I always end up having
to pick some up."
January 26, 2006
Photo by Wm. Glasheen

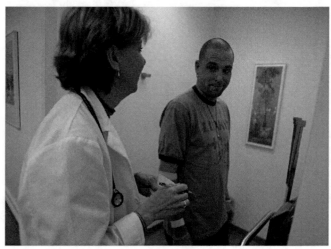

Stepping on the scale at the University of Wisconsin Madison hospital during a weekly visit.
Photo by Wm. Glasheen

Matt checks the weather before leaving for his weekly visit to the University
of Wisconsin Hospital in Madison, WI.
January 26, 2006
Photo for the Post Crescent by Wm. Glasheen

Matt walks past the main hospital entrance at the U. W. Hospital in Madison, WI on his way to the clinic where he will have lab work done, meet with his doctor, receive a transfusion of platelets and pick up his prescriptions.
January 26, 2006
Photo for the Post Crescent by Wm. Glasheen

Matt Morrell, center, cleans up during a game of poker with friends Jason Fournier, left, and Matt Peperkorn at Fournier's Darboy, WI, home.
January 22, 2006
Photo for the Post Crescent by Wm. Glasheen

Matt on the deck at his Oshkosh, WI, apartment.
Photo by Wm. Glasheen

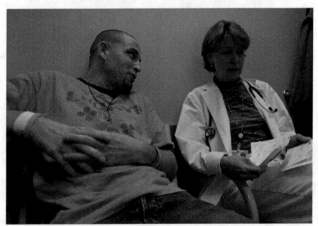

Matt teases Hematology Clinic RN Dawn Reininger as she hands him a half
dozen prescription refills following his visit with his doctor at the University of Wisconsin Hospital in Madison, WI.
January 26, 2006
Photo for the Post Crescent by Wm. Glasheen

Matt Morrell listens as his doctor talks to him about pain management during his weekly visit to the U.W. Hospital in Madison, WI.
January 26, 2006
Photo for the Post Crescent by Wm. Glasheen

Morrell walks down from the fifth floor of the parking garage to the clinic entrance at the University of Wisconsin hospital in Madison, WI. He always parks on the fifth floor and walks down. He jokes, "It's how I get my exercise."
January 26, 2006
Photo for the Post Crescent by Wm. Glasheen

FRIDAY, SEPTEMBER 23, 2005 12:17 AM, CDT
DAY 30—SHORT TANDEM REPEATING

"STR" or short tandem repeating … I bet there are a few people scratching their heads on this one, so I'll just keep it that way for awhile, as it's a funny sight in my head right now—Ha!!

The hospital was on my list of things to do today and was a very interesting, educational, and emotional day. I was placed in my normal Bay 29 in the high risk area of the chemotherapy section and jumped through all the normal hoops. Mattie was my nurse today and she advised me I had to play along today, as someone was shadowing her for the day. So I obliged and there was no copy and paste, but Mattie wrote nothing down, so realistically, it was!! Tracey came in to draw my blood and then I waited. Went and got some breakfast, read the USA Today, started a new book called "The Red Devil"—book about a cancer survivor—, watched my cooking show, and as "Days" started, Dr. Juckett came in for a visit.

My counts today were well and Dr. Juckett described my progress and how things were going as "stellar". My wbc is at 1900 with 1295 neutrophils, which means I am no longer neutropenic and less susceptible to infection. Platelets holding at 44,000, hemoglobin up to 11.2, rbc's up to 3,300, and magnesium just staying stubbornly at 1.4. Tacro levels not back yet, but was at 8 on Thursday, so holding well. So—where do we go from here?? The answer is "STR" or short tandem repeating.

"STR" is nothing more than DNA fingerprinting. Sure you are all relieved to know that and will feel good about yourself's for learning something new!! For those of you who knew, this will just be a quick synopsis. This is going to be a test performed next Tuesday and will take about 1 to 2 weeks to get back. This test will fingerprint my blood tests and immune system to see how the transplant is progressing. Dr. Juckett's prediction is this: Mark's cells should mostly be the wbc's, rbc's, and platelets—basically the marrow. The immune system cells should be mine. This test will be performed over the next 3 months to see how the transplant is working and after 3 months, the hope is that Mark has replaced everything. If his marrow and immune system has not, the transplant will not have worked. So—its an interesting test and I'm looking forward to it. He is also going to taper me off of the tacrolimus, as this will give Mark's immune system cells (T-Cells) a better chance to take over mine. This is also where GVHD comes into play. In essence, Dr. Juckett has gotten me out of the first set of woods and will place me into an unknown woods, which will be a different battle than the chemo woods, so I guess I'll have to buy a new pair of s*^t kickers.

That is where I stand and not much else to provide for the day, except that I am back in Appleton for the night, as Amy and I are heading down to Chicago tomorrow for the "Lucero" concert. Will be taking a day or two off from the journal to enjoy a mini-vacation!!! Don't worry though, as college football, NFL, and NASCAR reviews will shortly be upon you!!

I have two different sets of DNA right now and they are going to map it for me—for lack of better words, how neat!! I guess being sick sometimes does have its privileges, as I don't know anyone else who has an "STR" next week!! Simple Pleasures!!

MONDAY, SEPTEMBER 26, 2005 10:04 PM, CDT
DAY 31, 32, 33, 34—WORTH EVERY MINUTE

You can combine all of the days above and sum up it with three words, "Worth Every Minute" ... that is what it felt like to be in Chicago this weekend and to be out of Madison for a few days!! I drove back to Oshkosh on Thursday afternoon and took care of all the mail and business I have been amassing. That was sure a chore and Friday couldn't have come fast enough!!

We left for Chicago at 3:00 p.m., due to some change in plans due to having a whole week to get ready for it, and so I was a little frustrated to be stuck in the tail end of Milwaukee traffic and the middle of Chicago traffic. It only took us an hour and a half to go 13 miles, so I guess it wasn't too bad. We finally made it to the hotel—The Inn at Lincoln Park—and checked in. We made it up to the room about 6:45 p.m. and it was about 3 hours to go time!!

We left the hotel a bit after 8 p.m. and just started walking down Clark Street towards where the venue was. It was about a mile walk and we just thought we would find where it was and stop at a bar and grab some quick food. We found the "Bottom Lounge" where the show was and then ended up at "Trader Todd's". It was the only thing that was close by that we saw that was a bar/food joint. I hate karaoke and this place was karaoke 7 days a week!! Oh well—we would only be there for a little bit, so we joined the crowd. (They had a free shuttle to the Cubs game in a short bus, that had life preservers instead of seat belts. It was hilarious!! It was now 20 minutes to 10 p.m. and we left to go to the show.

We got to the show and stood in line to get in and finally, we were in the door!! The Chris Mills Band started off and they were pretty sweet—awesome lead singer—didn't buy any cd's as had to save my $$ for Lucero stuff and plus they play in Madison here to-morrow night, so that might have to make its way on the agenda!!!

Limbeck was next and they just rocked. It was a circus by the end of the show—they all had their shirts off for the last song and Chris Mills and Lucero joined them on stage and they all had their shirts off and they were jamming out and crazy string was going ev-erywhere and the stage was being sprayed with water and booze and they were all running into each other, all while still jamming on their instruments. It was awesome. I would definitely check out a Limbeck show if you get the chance.

Then came Lucero. It was just awesome. All it was cracked up to be and more. They played old stuff, they played new stuff, they played stuff I hadn't heard—it just rocked. So much energy, passion, feeling—it was almost haunting. I could see a show every night and not get sick of them—that's how their cd's are—hard to find that in a band these days. They had a "DVD" of like their first two years getting started, which would be like around late 1990's / early 2000/1 and they asked each band member what they sounded like—the lead singer said it best, "We're kind of music, that like, you're just driving down the high-way … yeah … like driving down the highway"—awesome!!

Crashed hard that night and Saturday we drove home, wishing we were going to another concert!! Crashed hard for the rest of the day and woke up to see Barry Alvarez being interviewed on ESPN2—Badgers over Michigan—unbelievable!!

Sunday was spent watching the NASCAR Race and watching Stewart struggle all day, finally catch a break, and then get caught in the pits when Kenseth brings out the yellow. I don't even know how NASCAR can look itself in the mirror while they allow Ford's to be raced. "The Chase" is getting interesting after two races here—think its going to come down to the last race—if anyone is going out to Vegas, I'll still take Stewart to win it, and would lay any amount you can afford to lay down in Vegas for me at the Bellagio. As for the Packers—I didn't see a play in the game, except Longwell kicking another Field Goal. I don't have much else to say!!

I drove back to reality today and am hitting the sack here, as my doctor appointment tomorrow starts at 7:30 a.m. with labs.

So—for my own attempt at advertising:

$80 for round-trip gas, $5 in tolls, $120 for a hotel room, $25 for tickets … Seeing "Lucero" live in concert in Chicago—Priceless.

WEDNESDAY, SEPTEMBER 28, 2005 12:24 AM, CDT
DAY 35—A SMALL WORLD SOMETIMES IT IS

I suppose that you could say that Part II of my journey here has begun. I had labs at the clinic today and then met with Dr. Juckett. One surprise—magnesium up to 1.5—almost normal!! Rest of the counts are just hanging at where they have been as of last week—not going up much and not going down much—low, but stable. So there wasn't too much to talk about on that level. Over the past week and a half or so, I've been getting these weird feelings that run from the back of my neck down into my stomach. I guess it feels like the feeling you are driving around in your car and all of a sudden someone pulls out of nowhere and you get that "Oh Sh*t" feeling—that quick adrenaline rush or something. I have been getting that through the day—no patterns—can be sitting, laying, standing, driving, etc. Dr. Juckett thinks it may be from the Tacro and some neurological changes and we are just going to watch it and see if it continues as I taper off Tacro. That is the other news—I am down to 1.5 milligrams for the next two weeks, 1mg the two weeks after that, and 0.5mg the fifth and sixth week. So again—here is the GVHD time frame starting. Also—counts are important as if they start dropping and not fluctuating, then it may not be working and the leukemia may be back. If the counts fluctuate, that means the bone marrow transformation is occurring. All in watching the counts and nothing to do until we see a trend!! Also had the "STR", so excited for those results. I go back in on Friday for labs and then again next Tuesday.

I'm going to skip the middle of the day, as I can't really remember my dreams and that's all I have to play on, so … continues due to length …

WEDNESDAY, SEPTEMBER 28, 2005 12:25 AM, CDT
DAY 35—A SMALL WORLD SOMETIMES IT IS CONT …

However this evening is a different story. I have a great story. OK here goes—so on Friday night in Chicago, the opening band was the Chris Mills band. We'll I thought I saw in the "Isthmus" that they were going to be in Madison before I left for Chicago. Well I checked when I came back this morning and low and behold—they were playing at the "Cafe Montmartre" tonight. It was only $7 to get in, so I thought, why the hell not. I thought they were sweet in Chicago, so why not see them in a smaller venue. So I decided to go to the show!!

I was talking on the phone with Korn as I arrived at the door, so I went around the corner to get out of the way and continue the conversation, when I saw Chris Mills also on the side of the building talking on his cell. I kind of nodded my head at him and he nodded his head back at me. Well—I was wearing the "Limbeck" shirt that I got this past weekend—and heard him say to who he was talking too, "Dude—someone has a Limbeck shirt on here" and I kind of laughed. I hung up with Korn and then Chris Mills came up to me and said, "I like your shirt". I said, "Thanks. I went to Chicago last weekend to see Lucero, walked out with a Limbeck shirt, and ended up coming to see you guys play again tonight, as I live here in Madison". He started laughing and said that was awesome. Then we both walked inside and I was geeked cause Chris Mills just came up and talked to me and he was geeked that he was making fans!! I felt kind of stupid seen as I was by myself, but whatever. I walked into this bar / cafe and took a seat at a table in the back by the sound guys, where the only other place to go was the kitchen!! They started the show late and let me tell you, that its kind of hard to kill 45 minutes sitting by yourself, except reading everything three times and pretending you are ready it for the first time!! HaHa—yes I can laugh at myself too.

Charlemagne played first and they were alright. Just before it was time for The Chris Mills Band to go on, he walked back by my table and told me, "I just got off the phone with Limbeck. They said thanks for wearing our shirt!!". Yeah—I'm kewl. Anyway—they came on stage and they just rocked. It was different than Chicago, as they had a horn / sax / piano player in Chicago, but they didn't here. Plus the place had like only 50 people in it and there couldn't have been more than 10 people who knew who this guy was. That was why it was so awesome. They played over an hour and it was just a blast. After the show, I bought one of his old cd's to have it in my collection with the new one, which doesn't hit stores until October 25th by the way, and we chatted for a minute, shook hands, and then out the door I went.

Then I had to deal with one of those computerized parking garages which are really convenient, but only after you learn how to use them, which isn't hard, just kind of a hassle!!

So point being—don't be afraid to do things on your own— it just might not be that bad!! And nothing beats live music at a small venue, when you know someone is going to one day be a big thing. Simple Pleasures and Stories—its what makes up life—Simple Pleasures and Stories—right Moth!!

WEDNESDAY, SEPTEMBER 28, 2005 11:23 PM, CDT
DAY 36—RAINED OUT AND RAINED IN

My day started early with a phone call at 5 a.m. from my friend Lucky, who was going to drive in from Milwaukee, as we had plans and a tee time to play University Ridge today. However, a look at the weather saw cold temps, rain, and 20 mph winds. We decided for a rain check—my second one I might add—and I feel I will have to play the Ridge by myself here before its too late for the year. So in lieu of the decision, I went back to bed and woke up with just enough time to make some coffee and turn on "Days"—rough I know and yes I make a mean cup of cowboy coffee.

But—caught up on my shows missed last night and played around on the computer. Didn't do anything worthwhile and kind of just took the day off.

Watched "Lost" and still trying to figure out the number sequence and then was entertained by "Invasion"—who doesn't like stories about "EBE's". Tweedle Dee and Tweedle Dumb.

But that's it for the day—needed a day off, took it, and look forward to seeing "Bascom Hill" tomorrow night with Korn:

www.bascomhillband.com

FRIDAY, SEPTEMBER 30, 2005 02:25 AM, CDT
DAY 37—LIVE MUSIC AND GOLDEN TEE

After such a long and excruciating day yesterday, I ended up sleeping in until close to noon today. I wasn't awoken by my alarm though cause I had that set much earlier so I would be sure to be up for "Days", so I don't know what happened there. What I do know, is that the cleaning people are on time, as they were here to clean my apartment at its regular scheduled time!!! I asked for a few minutes, got up, and got out as soon as I could!!

I ended up going to a book shop and then to Barnes and Noble and just read for a few hours. I headed back home around 4 p.m. and then got a call from Korn saying he would be here around 6 p.m., so I just kind of chilled out. Korn did arrive around 6 p.m. and we killed two hours watching our friend Chris Burks in a couple DVD videos in Iraq that he burnt for me while he was back in town the past few weeks. Speechless—saw some kewl things, saw some things that would need getting used to, and saw some things that make you smile!! Burks is going back over for a 4th deployment after the New Year here, so as always dude—keep your head up, shoot em before they shoot you, and I always got your back (as does everyone).

Around 8:30ish or so, Korn and I ventured to the High Noon Saloon, as "Bascom Hill" was playing. There were two other bands playing before them and there really wasn't that many people their, which disappointed me. The previous bands were sweet and during this time, Korn and I played two rounds of Golden Tee. For those of you who know Korn and I around a Golden Tee—I won!! Yeah—I won!! On a side note, Korn's brother, his wife, and Korn's girl friend or as we call her his "girlfriend", also was there. According to Kramer, there is an over / under of Korn moving to Minnesota by the end of October. Again—Kramer isn't real good at making good lines, so I'll take the over on that, but I guess there is still 31 days to see—hahahaha!! Korn's going to hate me, but I teased him about the October thing and he said, "But I haven't even kissed her yet!!!". I laughed my ass off, thought about a moth I saw earlier in the day, and continued to laugh at Korn's comment!! So at least Korn has a mission this weekend.

But back to the concert—my good luck with band members continued and I went up to talk to the lead singer, Charlie. Bascom Hill hung out with my friend Kate and Adam after their show in Chicago last Saturday, so Kate e-mailed me pictures of the show and said to go talk to him, so I did. It was pretty kewl—we talked for a few minutes before they went on and they are going to be playing at "Tom's Garage" in Appleton in a few weeks, so for everyone in the area—go check them out. Another day, another simple pleasure and story.

If anyone of you read the guestbook each day, please keep Bill and his family in your thoughts and Corey and his family in your thoughts. I can honestly say that its hard being out of the hospital and knowing other people who are still in. Even though our transplants are completely different, I can't help but feel guilty that I'm out at concerts and he's barely able to eat. You almost want to switch positions—even just for a day—I don't know—it's tough—I've known the feeling of being told you can go home and then you can't—I can only explain it in words that shouldn't be typed out here. It's tough.

Tomorrow I go back in for labs early in the morning and don't even have to stick around. They will call with any problems with the counts, so they just keep moving me along the process at a rate I'm sure no one expected!!

Long night and quick day coming, but simple pleasures and stories trump that anytime.

SATURDAY, OCTOBER 01, 2005 05:34 PM, CDT
DAY 38 AND 39—MUCH ADO ABOUT NOTHING

Well I haven't heard anything from the hospital yet, so that must mean that my lab tests from Friday are just fine. I had my blood drawn and then was allowed to leave, which I don't quite mind at all!! It was a good thing though, as Korn and I had a round of golf to get too.

We played Yahara Hills and it wasn't too bad of a course. It reminds me of Mid-Vallee out towards DePere. They have 38 holes to play and we played the east course. Was still in great shape, with the normal winter kill most courses received last year. Had a few good holes, struggled around the green, and wish my score was written in invisible ink. Korn had a good day as usual—firing an 88. We had about 3 holes with the wind at our backs and Korn must have crushed each one of those drives close to 300 yards—you see something like that and then you think about Tiger who can hit it 400 sometimes and its just like, whatever!!

Didn't do much on Friday except watch some TV and finish reading the "Red Devil". Think I will tackle "American Caesar" next—bio about Gen. MacArthur or an Abraham Lincoln bio—"The Living Lincoln". Hamilton could soon follow, but …

Today I made myself useful and did my laundry—was smart this time and saved the open washers by placing 4 quarters on top with a sticky note saying "be right back". It worked!! Watched MI squeak out a victory, NY clinch the AL East, and Penn State is crushing MN. Glad to see one team may be for real after playing a schedule that would see the "Sisters of the Blind" at 2-2. Still think Penn St. is a joke, but we'll see.

Wanted to let you all know that tomorrow is the 3rd race in the "Chase for the Cup". Why is this week so special—it's at Talladega Motor Speedway—my favorite track and favorite race to watch on TV. We'll see if NASCAR lets Jimmy Johnson and Kyle Busch continue to have higher cars than anyone else and get a slap on the wrist, while Kevin Harvick's team forgets to close a stupid vent door in the trunk and the crew chief is suspended again. Politics here, Politics there, just follow the money to Tom Delay. I suspect two members of the state of WI's political arena aren't surprised. But anyway—back to NASCAR—Talladega at 12:30 central on NBC!! (I feel like an advertising campaign here sometimes—Boston / NY on ESPN at 1 p.m.—NFL on local channels all day).

Nothing on tap for tonight, so I'm sure it will be a blockbuster of a time. See more advertising.

MONDAY, OCTOBER 03, 2005 03:17 AM, CDT
DAY 40—HAPPY BIRTHDAY TO ANYONE OF THIS AGE TODAY!!

For all week, nothing has been more prevalent on my mind than who the Braves and Red Sox will face in the Playoffs and how many "Big Ones" would happen at Talladega Motor Speedway!! An e-mail I read this morning changed my whole perspective for the day, but a conversation later in the evening reminded me that Simple Pleasures really are the key to life. So with that in mind ...

Talladega was phenomenal. I hope that Jimmie Johnson gets taken out of each and every race the next 7 races. I hope someone finds a way to bump draft him behind the wall after 20 laps and then maybe he will really have something to whine about. The "Big One" came at 20 laps and took out a slew of the field, including Dale Jr. and Michael Waltrip, who took a wild ride, seeming to fly in the air for two full rotations and landing on what was left of his four wheels. Not to be outdone though, Ryan Newman decided to try bump drafting in the corner one more time, only to cause "The Big One 2" and see Scott Riggs crush Waltrip in Style Points. To bad racing isn't figure skating, as a few 10's were certainly available to be given out. Newman I'll give a break to—he's been on the receiving end of so much bad luck, that he deserves a free pass. But most important, besides the fans cheering when Johnson was finally forced to call it quits, was the last 11 laps could have been the most exciting laps of the season. Awesome!! DJ takes the lead from Stewart on the last lap in what was just a crazy move on both Stewart and DJ's part and leaves Kenseth, Newman, and McMurray with a look of what just happened!! Stewart finishes second and takes over possession of the 1st place in the standings for the "Cup". Seven races to go—I'm pumped!! C'mon "Smoke".

To answer the other questions—Boston will be playing Chicago, which I think works out in their favor in a 5 game series. Atlanta will get the Astros again in a 5 game series, which is what all Brave fans wanted to see as revenge is a dish best served cold and with an Andrew Jones homer in your mug!! October only trails March as the best months of the year!!

Kramer continues to be crushed in Fantasy Football, as my VP16 team sent the New Orleans Storm Surge to their 4 straight defeat—all while keeping Plaxico Burress on the bench. Offered Kramer a trade for him, but he was so in shock at a devastating 4th defeat, that he may just be throwing in the towel already. At least he has an awesome TV to keep track of his players woes though!! Good Luck Next Week.

The "West Wing" continues to be my favorite show on TV, followed closely by "Days of Our Lives"—yes sometimes I wonder where my priorities are, but I swear they are no further away than an intense game of Jenga.

My advice for the day is for everyone to get in touch with a long lost friend, get rid of the moth balls, and find out what you've missed. My guess would be that it just may make your day, but then I'm just guessing, and we all know the results of that ;-)

TUESDAY, OCTOBER 04, 2005 01:29 AM, CDT
DAY 41—8 TEAMS 11 WINS AWAY FROM IMMORTALITY

The Green Bay Packers are the best 0-4 team in the NFL. Hands Down. In fact, they are the only 0-4 team in the NFL. Funny how that works. But you know what—I'm not ripping on the team—I'm ripping on the coaches. They aren't going to win with Sherman at the helms. They aren't going to win with the defense hitting wide receivers on the head before the ball is barely thrown. They aren't going to win when 3 wide receivers running the same route. Favre was unreal today—tough when you score 29 points and lose. I guess all I am saying is that the Packers need a direction and they don't have one—that starts from the top period. But they very well may win the Division at 6-10.

But with that out of the way, a pretty boring day on my end. Made it outside for about 30 minutes today, missed most of "Days" due to oversleeping (how can someone keep hitting snooze at noon?), and spent most of the day on the Internet looking at Wall Street.

The best realization of today, is that tomorrow the MLB Playoffs begin!! Pick up some new hats, break in the bills or give them to me to do, and let the games begin. I'm making the predictions here and will consider any wager one may be interested in. Boston over Chicago in 4. Anaheim over New York in 5. Atlanta over Houston in 4. St. Louis over San Diego in 3. Boston over Anaheim in 7. Atlanta over St. Louis in 7. And then my heart gets torn when Boston and Atlanta meet for the World Series. To see Boston take 2 in a row would be sweet. But the Braves are my team and they win in 7. Its been 10 years since the Braves hoisted a trophy (with Fred McGriff at first base!!!) and they match that glory this year!! Can't wait to see what magic will forever be indebted into my memory this year and for all you Yankee fans out there (more specifically Scully's wife Karen), I am laughing and basking in your heartache already!!!!! Can't wait for the calls to begin!!

As for the reason I even have this site, I go into the clinic tomorrow for labs and a visit with Dr. Juckett. Will see where my counts are at from last Friday and for tomorrow. Have nothing new to report to him and hope he might have more of an idea for the weird feelings running down my spine, which still haven't ceased. Maybe its just a side effect of too much key lime pie or that $1 bet I won for swallowing a "live" moth is coming back to haunt me.

I hope everyone has a chance to catch the Playoffs which start at 1 p.m. eastern time. If you are in a position where you can't watch the games, I have perfected a system of running a concealed cord, from a concealed transmission source on your pants, up your chest, down your arm, and ending up in the palm of your hand. This is a surefire way to catch all the play by plays, but standing up and cheering out loud, will give you away in classes and at work and may get you fired if it happens during an important meeting. But priorities are priorities and that should overcome any fear one might be feeling. (This same system and outcomes are well used in March as well).

I wanted to wish Julio Maya Racers, from the "Redneck Racing League", a quick recovery and hoping the "reduction" in points between Relli Racing 2 and your team end after this past weekend!! Recover with a piece of Key Lime Pie and keep saving your money to ship me a full pie in 7 weeks ;-)

And Finally: To walk off homers, to blown saves, to 40 year old pitching studs, to fan interference, to A-Rod trying to raise his postseason average to over .200, to heartaches, to jumping off the couch in excitement, to rally monkeys, to tomahawk chops, to finding the next Carlos Beltran in Houston, to hoping Rivera performs as well as last year, to hopes of calling Scully after a monster play, if only to talk to Karen, to Big Papi, to extra innings, to the fan cam, to the privilege of watching Jeter turning 2 (not all Yankees are bad—right Sheff), to Fergy in St. Louis having to watch Renteria playing all year in Boston, to a long distance high five to Jeremy in Michigan as A. Jones roams the outfield, to E. George and wishing we could spend the playoffs at the "Wooden Nickel" while you complain about the Reds, to San Diego finishing two games over .500, to the part that never fails to bring a tear in "Field of Dreams" and to 8 teams trying to win 11 games, Fergy "Yeah"—This Bud's for you!!

TUESDAY, OCTOBER 04, 2005 10:56 PM, CDT
DAY 42—5 WEEKS AND COUNTING ...

Five weeks—Sometimes I think I'm just like the Energizer Bunny—I keep going and going and going!! I went in for my weekly checkup with Dr. Juckett and things are going well and we are seeing some things that we wanted to see. My counts are fluctuating and my platelets dropped from Friday, my hemoglobin was the same, and magnesium and wbc's went up. He expects to see my counts continue to fluctuate and he advised me that I may bottom out again when Mark's cells become more aggressive, which could mean more transfusions and back in high risk. The DNA test should come back buy the end of the week or when I see him again next week Tuesday, so excited for that. It will be a good indicator of what to expect.

We also talked about the small problem I have been having. Decided to watch it again for another week, as he took me off of Fluconazale to see if that helps. If it doesn't help, it sounds as if there may be a problem with my heart and they will do some tests next week. But we will see how this week goes.

Not sure if many of you heard about the new study and tests that Stanford has been doing regarding bone marrow transplants, but they have found a way to lower the probability of GVHD, by separating the immune during the transplant. Dr. Juckett was surprised when he heard about it and said that everyone will remain a bit skeptical until more tests are proven on different ages and subjects, but it looks promising. The U of WI transplant staff was actually having a meeting on it later this afternoon and I guess that how it works has been around for years, its just someone finally came up with a way to combine the two treatments. So the outlook for future bone marrow transplants looks bright on the horizon.

I also have a huge announcement to make. I urge everyone to pick up the latest copy of Sports Illustrated and turn to the NHL Previews. I would like everyone to see that Sports Illustrated has picked the one and only CALGARY FLAMES to win the 2005/2006 Stanley Cup!! Why do I feel another trip to Calgary for a Playoff

Game in my future!! On a side note, the season starts tomorrow night and for those of us who are fans, its about damn time.

The Playoffs went a bit different than I hoped for and they were kind of boring games. Reggie Sanders with 6 RBI's—are you serious. I don't care if San Diego stagged a weak rally in the end, they are done. Chicago decided to score all the runs they are going to score in the series today, so Boston just decided to take the day off and we'll see Posednik and the BoSox return to earth tomorrow. I like the Angels chances. Two 2 out rally's hurt, but that was all they had. Glad to see A-Rod continue to struggle—wonder how much of his 256 million dollars he would give to be able to get a hit in the play-offs—guess that's just karma though A-Rod. Rivera struggled, but there is nothing like seeing him breaking bats in October. The Angels need a win, but I'm not panicking. Houston and Atlanta tomorrow. (Game 2 of this series sees Clemens vs. Smoltz on Thursday night, so Game 1 is huge).

That's all I've got. Surprised with so few playoff reactions posted, but maybe that means everyone agrees with me (except K.T.—I would bet on your picks too!!). To a long day of baseball tomorrow—Ciao.

WEDNESDAY, OCTOBER 05, 2005 11:44 PM, CDT
DAY 43—THREE TIMES A CHARM

Not to disappoint anyone, but maybe there was a reason Chris K. decided to leave me three messages on why he hated the Braves. I had a huge rebuttal, one that explained my position and then offered hope to Chris, as the Angels tied the game up as I was writing the journal and I wanted to tell him that routing for the Angels, but realistically thinking the Yankees will win, is not realistic, but giving up.

I went on about the beatings I took in the Playoffs and NHL tonight and had my regular "Lost" comment and how I was wondering where the guy Jack already new, was running to—I said "Into the season finale".

But I had a great entry—it didn't post. I was upset. I wrote another entry that was even better—that didn't post. Good thing I know how to copy and paste. Now I am on entry number three and I am way too exhausted to make a spectacle today, as I previously tried and failed due to my internet connection. So I am going to take the Simple Pleasure of typing number 3 and knowing 3 is a charm, so I should be alright here this time.

I will say to Chris K. though—The Angels just went up 4-2 vs. the Yankees. You can still hop on the bandwagon, but only if you believe. I'll let you back on and forget the "realistic" remark. A-Rod is E-5 Rod and that's all you need—just a chance!!

I'm fine—stopping flucon. hasn't helped the problem. I am feeling more tired this week than previous and have started napping again. Not a big fan of fluctuating counts.

This condensed version sucks, but I need some sleep. The cleaning people come early tomorrow and I have to be gone—guess I'll go to McDonalds and get breakfast, play Monopoly, read the paper, go back to McD's for lunch and Monopoly, and then go home in time for "Days". Boy what a busy morning. For those of you in my training class at Thrivent—yep—everyday!! Won a free drink and got a $3 best buy buck today!!

PS—Smoltz vs. Clemens tomorrow and Happy B-Day Korn!!

FRIDAY, OCTOBER 07, 2005 01:10 AM, CDT
DAY 44—BRAVES BOUNCE BACK

How about those Atlanta Braves??!! I don't know if Clemens wanted to smile and tip his cap to Brian McCann or strangle him— the postseason and its wonders!! Smoltz got out of the 1st and was untouchable—just like the good ole days. I see the veteran leadership and the smiles on the young kids faces and I can't help but feel something's going to happen—Oswalt vs. Sosa—two very hot pitchers in September. Could be the Clemens vs. Smoltz game we were all expecting tonight … Cards continue their roller coaster ride over the Padres, who are just happy to be in the playoffs. Won't win anything just being happy your new stadium gets to host a playoff game. Notice I said game. Angles need Chris K. on their side to continue vs. New York and Boston just needs to find a pulse or its "goat and hero" parade is over … C'mon Big Papi!!

Seen as I'm not going to the doctor but weekly, I'm running out of things to say, except for creating my own little blog here. But I don't have much to say tonight, except I really hope the leader of the free world isn't listening to voices in his head and making the decisions of our time. Wonder how dear old dad is going to let the White House spin this—can't wait for tomorrow's political cartoons. They usually are good for a laugh and a hint of the truth. That's just my take though—All we need is a slumping economy with a poor outlook, the Feds raising rates, and Bush taking orders from someone called God—I'm just curious which one, as our religious tolerance gives him a choice of about 22 different Gods, but I'll have to have Amy confirm that from her "Religions in America" class notes from last semester. I sense a nail in the coffin of his legacy.

To end, I recommend purchasing the new "Nickelback" CD and the new "Shinedown" CD for those who enjoy a little noise—they rock!!

Remember—I'll be here all week. Your questions and comments are welcome anytime. PS—I got Park Place today—just need to find Boardwalk.

SUNDAY, OCTOBER 09, 2005 01:46 AM, CDT
DAY 45 AND 46—JOURNAL DELAYED DUE TO MOURNING

Friday afternoon soured my mood and ambition for the day, as I listened to the Red Sox give away another ball game, thus losing all hopes and chances for a repeat World Series. To do so to a Chicago White Sox team that played so poorly at the end of the year, was just too much to take for this sportswriter/fan. That was only the third playoff series the Sox have won since 1917, so I guess I will tip my hat to them and concede a lose on my predictions. I will now have to change my predictions and say Anaheim over Chicago in 6. I know the Angels haven't won there series against NY yet, but that is only because they were rained out today. Wonder if George is re-thinking his Randy Johnson signing?

The only other comment I had to make on Friday, was to give a shout out to my Calgary Flames and let everyone know that they picked up their first win of the season—one of too many to count right now!!

Anyway—the Cardinals pulled through for me and I called that sweep. I didn't call Reggie Sanders have a NLDS record 10 rbi's, but who would have. Cardinals look tough—but then when don't they?

College Football today was interesting—WI looked like the Packers—MN pulled off what MI State couldn't—Joe Paterno just might be back—TN needs to quit turning over the ball—Texas had a long time coming—USC is going to get beat here by UCLA if they keep playing like they have already won the National Championship and only show up to play one half of football.

The Braves just couldn't pull out the comeback and have their backs against the fence, just like last year. They will pull off a win tomorrow and bring it back to Atlanta for game 5. St. Louis coasts to a rest and Anaheim (Sorry—L.A. Angels) may have the 2nd surprise of the postseason up their sleeves.

Had the fortune of going to the Badger Hockey Game vs. St. Lawrence. The Kohl Center is one sweet place. The Badgers should have won, but there wasn't much 5 on 5. They had too many penalties and a costly 5 minute major with 12 minutes in the 3rd by Earl, gave St. Lawrence a power play goal. Even though St. Lawrence had only one power play goal, they had one of the best power plays I have seen run in a long time. Awesome to watch—the Badgers only let one player shoot and you could defend it with three people all day long and not worry about a thing the way they ran it. St. Lawrence scored 14 seconds into OT on a nice face off and offensive zone play.

Man—it sounds like I have nothing to do but analyze sports all day long. Funny how I did that anyway!! Tomorrow is going to be one long day and I am glad that I finally have cable installed!!! There are three Playoff Games, the regular NFL games, and the NASCAR race at Kansas. I told Amy that we have to get up early tomorrow, so that I can go to the store and get a cable splitter. We are going to take both bedroom TV's and bring them into the living room for a few hours—one on the Race, one of the Playoffs, and one on Football. Sound on the Race—nothing like hearing that all day!!!

So with that said, I need to get some rest for a long day tomorrow!! Feeling okay the last two days—started needing some naps again, but all this sporting actions is wearing me out!! Strap your seat belt on—tomorrow is going to be a crazy day!!

SUNDAY, OCTOBER 09, 2005 11:15 PM, CDT
DAY 47—(*^*&$&^*&)_)()(*(*&*&^&^$^%#

Today could have been one of the most exciting days in sports Sunday history ever. But I will start off by saying this, "If I ever sit down and watch an 18 inning baseball game again and it involves the Braves and they lose in the playoffs one more time, I will say the following words I used today (*^&$&^*&))()((*&*&^&^$^%# and never watch another Brave Playoff game again". Of course I am lying, but unreal. I could go on and on and on, but will just leave it with the above words.

To rewind a bit though, today took a bit of preparation. I woke up early and traveled to Wal-Mart to pick up a cable splitter. I got home and woke Amy up and said we need to eat now or we won't have time. She didn't know what I was going to do, although she had an idea. So we went and ate breakfast and came back to the apartment. I took both TV's out of the respective bedrooms and dusted 5 years of dust off them. Then I had to move the desk from the guest bedroom out into the living room. From there, I placed the other two TV's on top of the desk and hooked everything up via cable splitter. It was just awesome. I had the Packer Game on the left TV, the race on the middle TV, and the baseball game on the right TV.

The Packer game had sound for an hour—then the race had sound for four and a half hours—then the baseball game had sound for 2 hours. It was just awesome. I haven't moved from the couch except to go to the bathroom and that makes 11 hours watching sports and it just ended with the Bengal game. Amy just couldn't handle it when I flipped over to golf when Tiger and Daly had it out in playoffs and I commented on Tiger's shot, cheered for a Braves double play and then shouted fumble in less than 30 seconds. Awesome!! I didn't' miss a thing today, but do wish I would have.

I just don't have it in my heart to cheer the Astros, especially after Farnsworth blew the game. The Astros were 15 games under .500 in June and they win the wild card—unreal. What a game though!! For those who watched it, we watched history today—the longest game in postseason history and it could stay that way my whole life!! Like I said yesterday—the Packers and Badgers switched spots for the weekend. Tony Stewart takes 4th and has a stranglehold on the "Chase for the Cup". Indy remains the only unbeaten football team and my pick to start A. Brooks as my quarterback wasn't such a good idea. Tiger pulled one out, as Daly reminds us that maybe we aren't so bad after all. Piss off Astros and Yankees—back to LA for game 5 tomorrow night!!! I need the Angels to at least go 2 for 4 in my predictions!!! The Flames got crushed by Detroit tonight and are slowly making there way back to Calgary after the season starts with 4 road games. Think that's enough to chew on for now. Its funny—I just shut off Sportscenter—its the first time I have been able to watch it in over a month and there isn't anything new on there I haven't seen 10 times today already!!!

I do have pictures of my fiasco today and plan to post one or two as soon as I use up my film. I do believe that with so much going on for at least another two weeks, I have re-arranged my apartment for awhile. (I did take an hour break from sports, leaving one TV on Mute with the Yankees game and turning the other two on the West Wing—that was fun to watch!!).

A bit sensory overloaded here, but feeling okay. Big day on Tuesday, so just trying to kill time until then. Hope everyone had an enjoyable day today and have a good week at work—I'll keep tabs on anything developing in any major sports market and let you know tomorrow night.

PS—To the only important matter of the day though, for all of those who visit my site and are familiar with the name Megan Eklund, who also went to Neenah High School, please visit her caringbridge site and keep her in your thoughts and prayers, as she continues to fight her battle against cancer with the same intensity, emotion, and tenacity that I have:

http://www2.caringbridge.org/az/meganeklund/index.htm

Power Button Off, Off, Off.

MONDAY, OCTOBER 10, 2005 11:24 PM, CDT
DAY 48—WELCOME NEW YORK TO "NEXT YEAR'S" FAN CLUB

It's always easier to handle the defeat of your team, when the team you hate the most, also falls in the postseason. The World Series this year will be decided west of the Mississippi and I just don't know who to route for now—guess its back to wishing every game has a hero in the bottom of the 9th or something crazy like that. I was .500 on my predictions, so its time to up that average. You know—I could not make a correct prediction the rest of the Playoffs and still have a better average than A-Rod—hahahahahaha—he's so far down, he can't even see the Mendoza line—maybe another team will pay you more and you can try your luck there.

I have an update on the Bloedorn family that I met when I was in the hospital—Bill was in receiving a transplant and his wife Jean, was in receiving treatments for colo-rectal cancer. Bill is doing okay—out of the hospital, but presented today with GVHD. They put him on prednisone and are now very closely watching if it gets better or worse. (This is expected after transplants and how it is controlled, is the key to how you fare). Unfortunately, his wife Jean found out that she has cancer in different areas than what she is currently being treated for. She is undergoing a liver biopsy to see if one area on the liver is cancer or not. She is facing a tough road ahead, but if her biopsy comes back negative, she has a potential chance for a cure, if the new regime of chemo they are going to try, works. Please keep Bill, Jean, Tanya, and all of the family in your thoughts and prayers. You might be able to catch them at the River Rail one night—so I have them looking for you Tom and Cindee!!!!

Pretty quiet today and for once in my life, looking forward to going to the doctor tomorrow. DNA fingerprinting—amazing every time I think about it!!

PS—new book night tonight. The "Living Lincoln" completed and available for interested readers.

WEDNESDAY, OCTOBER 12, 2005 02:48 AM, CDT
DAY 49—SEVEN WEEKS AND MY ROAD IS JUST STARTING—COME WILL WHAT MAY.

Happy 7 Week Anniversary to me, Happy 7 Week Anniversary to me, Happy 7 Week Anniversary to me … Happy 7 Week Anniversary to me!!

Seriously though—I received a lot of information today and its pretty confusing, so I will try to keep it simple and less technical. To start, a "mini-transplant" is a transplant that is still in its pioneering stages. The regime has changed, who and what they treat are changing, and long term effects and studies are only now coming back and being useful in treating people pre and post transplant. With that said—

A mini-transplant patient is put on tacrolimus and then they are tapered off of it, in order for the transfusion to fully take over. It is when the new system fully takes over (or close to taking over) that the GVHD becomes present. As of a study out of Seattle, people tapered off between days 28-56 are developing chronic GVHD around day 100 to day 180 and they are developing incurable chronic GVHD and there is a high mortality rate. Those tapered off between day 56 to 100 are showing slight improvements and those tapered off between day 100 and day 180, show improvement upon that. Its necessary to understand this before I can explain my situation clearly.

Before today, I was to have been tapered off of tacro w/in the next four weeks or what would have amounted to 76 days. As of today, that has been changed and I will not taper off of tacro over the next 3 months. This should bring my total to 157 days until I am off tacro. We are trying to delay the onset of the GVHD and hope that waiting longer, prevents a chronic occurrence.

With that being said, I can announce that as for my DNA Fingerprinting, I am showing 80% Mark and 20% Matt. This is a very good figure, but now one that we are going to try to hold and very slowly improve over the next 3 months. The problem with this route, is that keeping part of my system around, gives the leukemia a chance to come back before we rid myself of all of my cells. So its kind of a trade off based on the studies and statistics … cont.

WEDNESDAY, OCTOBER 12, 2005 02:49 AM, CDT
DAY 49: SEVEN WEEKS AND MY ROAD IS JUST STARTING… CONT

What this all means, is that I am stable enough to go home within the next few weeks. I still will be followed each week and in two months, will have another DNA test and a bone marrow biopsy to check things. So—even though I am getting better in the short term here, I will have the major battle to fight in a few months. Time frame shows around December / January or the time I approach being out 180 days post transplant.

Today's meeting can be summed up with the following: I made a statement to Dr. Juckett, stating that according to our plan now and what the future holds, that I'm no where close to being out of the woods—his reply was that we have really just stepped in.

However—we did know this from the beginning. We were aware of the fact that if I made it past chemo, that I would get out and get better and then would at some point, get worse again and that would be the major fight. Due to how well I was doing, Dr. Juckett was speeding some things up, as we felt comfortable doing that. With the new data and studies released, that route is no longer the safest. We all know that I am not one for statistics and only relate to them for people to understand. The only statistic that matters, is which stat I become. However with that being said, I have full faith in Dr. Juckett and do not disagree with him about the plan of action. I said from the start that if he was willing to attempt the transplant, that I would be the guinea pig and do what he said. That's the faith that I believe in and what I have in my situation.

We are also going to wait another week on the heart issues, to see if increasing the tacro relates to anything or not. My counts are also slowly rising from last time and the only thing to drop, was the magnesium at 1.4. Surprise, Surprise!!

So that is what I can relate as far as now. I know it is hard to understand and follow. The easiest way would simply be to know that I am doing OK right now and that I have a long road ahead of me, as even though we have a plan, plans tend to change!!

On another note—the Angels did beat the White Sox tonight and I couldn't be happier about it. Lucky, Mike, and Tim made it down to Madison today around 9 p.m. As instructed to relay to Korn—I won both rounds of cards we played. Mike couldn't win a hand, Lucky was easy money, and I had Tim's number twice head to head. Had to clear some cash out of the playing chips so the case would close!!!! We are getting psyched for a round at University Ridge tomorrow and I wish I was sleeping right now, but I can't and I don't think throwing any other pill into my body will do it any good at this hour. If anyone is up reading this—give me a call—its 2:45 a.m., I have to be up in 4 hours, but think it may take me that long to fall asleep!!

Tomorrow will be full of simple pleasures and days like that bring smiles and saneness. Out.

THURSDAY, OCTOBER 13, 2005 05:39 PM, CDT
DAY 50, 51, 52, 53, 54, 55, AND 56: VACATION

The Author of this website has cited creative differences and lack of a decent paying contract with management, therefore leading to an unpaid leave of absence. Agents for both parties will be meeting extensively during MLB Playoff Action the next few days and hope to have a signed contract in place by the end of the Ohio State vs. Michigan State, Wisconsin vs. Minnesota, Texas vs. Colorado, or USC vs. Notre Dame game.

If negotiations break down at any point during the weekend, both parties have expressed that they will take Saturday night off to watch Tony "2005 "Chase for the Cup" Champion" Stewart at Lowe's Motor Speedway, where they are hoping annual favorite Jimmie Johnson wrecks in lap 20, and will continue talks during the Sunday NFL action where the only action, will be coming from the

Minnesota "That's Crazy. Sex? Come On" Vikings travel to Chicago for a battle of 1-3 teams. Sweet—Ratings ought to soar thinks Fox.

Before heading for leave, the author did leave a statement: "May everyone learn a lesson from L.A. Angels manager Mike Scioscia, who showed that grace can be shown under fire and under losing. What happens in the human element happens and as Scioscia said, "We just didn't play at a high enough level to win tonight". Class—pure class.

WEDNESDAY, OCTOBER 19, 2005 01:52 PM, CDT
DAY 57, 58, 59, 60, 61: CONTRACT ISSUES RESOLVED AND AUTHOR RETURN EXPECTED LATER THIS EVENING ...

MONDAY, OCTOBER 24, 2005 11:57 PM, CDT
DAY 62: THANKS JAMMIE

Unbelievable—take one trip out of country, have a little fun, and next thing you know, you're stuck in Customs for 5 days without a phone call, but for some reason this time I was fed. Believe I only was given water last time, but those days are a bit hazy now!!

But, I can honestly say this time that I am safely in the comfort of the United States and able to get back to catching up with this journal of mine, that has been pushed aside for a few reasons, none which hold much credibility with the public, so I won't even attempt to use them and see my approval rating be in competition with someone else I am familiar with!!

I have not been feeling well as of lately and go back to the doctors tomorrow. I'm sure its all relative and the wonderful change of seasons—October has just not been my month the last 4 years and I am one more episode away from adding this October to that list—fairly confident that will happen tomorrow, but I'll let you know then!!

Thank you everyone for all of your support and thank you to Jammie for the touching posting and I will be at work tomorrow in the late afternoon, so I'll stop by and say "HI".

WEDNESDAY, OCTOBER 26, 2005 11:39 AM, CDT
DAY 63 AND 64: JUST DRIVING AROUND

If I were to sum up the last few days, it would take more space than I have, so I will keep it simple, use poor sentence structure, and small words: One of my good friends came back from Iraq for a few days and drove up to Oshkosh on Thursday, which was a fun night. He and his girlfriend (from Calgary I might add) left Friday morning and I did some cleaning around the apartment in Oshkosh. Went out to eat Friday night and Saturday morning, as my Dad was in town. Later Saturday morning, I started not feeling well. Still don't feel that well, but better each day this week.

On Friday I received news that my long term disability had been denied and on Monday, I received the letter. I was also sent an e-mail that said Thrivent would be terminating my position, which meant I had no insurance, death benefits, etc. Not thrilled. Talked with Thrivent and had a meeting setup for Tuesday. Drove down to Madison on Monday night, slept, and went to the doctor's on Tuesday. Dr. Juckett was a little concerned with how I was feeling. Said I may have just caught a cold, couldn't really explain the bone pain except for the marrow acting up or such, so he took some blood and is running another "DNA" test to see. I showed him my denial letter and he got social services involved. I talked with Neil and he advised me what steps to take.

So—Tuesday afternoon I drove back up to Appleton to have my meeting at Thrivent. This went well, as I advised them I was writing an appeal, filing a complaint, etc,etc. They then offered to put me on unpaid leave, which would mean I was still technically an employee. I will pay my insurance premiums from out of pocket, as which were previously paid via paycheck, but I no longer receive one of those, as my Short Term Disability ran out on Monday. This will keep my insurance, death benefits, etc until the appeal process is done. After that time, I will either won and be placed on long term disability or lost and be faced with Cobra. Nothing is ever easy is it?

So there is a quick catchup. Houston needs a miracle—they just can't win right now. Its amazing how they look unbeatable at times and then self destruct. Wow—I'm still rooting for them though—all they have to do is win four games. One of the teams has to!!

It sure is getting cold out around here, so make sure to set those final tee times for Saturday—should be a beautiful day to spend outside!!

THURSDAY, OCTOBER 27, 2005 11:23 PM, CDT
DAY 65 AND 66: HISTORY

There is nothing like watching a team celebrate the winning of a championship. With that, I couldn't help but feel like a little kid with goose bumps, as Chicago stormed the field to celebrate an amazing Post-Season Run by Winning the 2005 MLB World Series. You can't help but smile when you watch tears of joy running down faces of the Chicago players and you can't help but drop a tear when you see tears of lost opportunities running down faces of the Houston Astros. Was it the greatest World Series ever—not even close. Will some of us struggle to remember in 10 years who won the World Series in 2005? Unfortunately yes. Either way—for whoever watched the end, saw yet another moment of history in their lifetimes that will forever be remembered long after we are gone. That in itself is a feeling entirely different!!

Other than that—not too much here. I will have to say that anyone who says that "George W. Bush is the smartest person I have met", does not have the qualifications to be a Supreme Court Justice. It is nice to see the system of checks and balances work in a time when all satire aside, a choice really does not fit. Not too sure when George Senior and Barbara became die-hard Houston fans, but I'm just not too sure I could pull that off and sit behind home plate and keep score. Some things never cease to amaze me.

Today I had the humbling experience of playing a round of golf at North Shore in Menasha. Simply beautiful scenery and an interesting course to play. The weather was nice and fair for October, but I think my clubs and golf balls like it a bit warmer, as they weren't too kind to the course today, but they did take the time to visit 70% of the trees and sand traps, so that was nice of them. A genuine thanks to Mr. Mason for lunch, conversation, 18, and ship, captain, crew. Much Appreciated.

To end—Virginia Tech may very well have a say at who deserves to be #1 by the time January rolls around. Marcus is no Michael, but Frankie B. is still the man.

MONDAY, OCTOBER 31, 2005 12:30 AM, CST
DAY 67,68, AND 69: LOSE A BATTLE TO WIN A WAR

Atlanta Motor Speedway is usually a decent race to watch for entertainment purposes. Today was not one of those days. It was going to come down to whoever had the car at the time. Martin had it, Junior had it, Gordon looked tough, Stewart was solid (thanks for the 5 points Jr) and then here comes Mr. (I have something up my sleeve) Edwards to take back to back wins at Atlanta. The kid is good. Just wish he didn't race a Ford!! But when all is said and done, Tony Stewart takes an interesting 43 point lead. I say interesting because it is like a 2-0 lead in hockey. It can shrink to 2-1 in a heartbeat or become a demanding 3-0 lead. Three left to go and I think Texas next week is the most important. As he said, "Today I had to lose the battle to win the war". Simple words from the 2005 NASCAR Nextel Cup Champion in three weeks.

Not too much to comment on really. College football had no huge games or upsets, unless you count Florida beating a devastated Georgia team with no quarterback. Gotta love statistic building games against Illinois and Texas waiting until the second half to bury OK. State again.

Not real happy with the NFL this weekend, as I was taken out in my "three and out" pool this week. I took Dallas and Tampa Bay. Dallas was a lock and why wouldn't Tampa Bay? They are 5-1, have SF starting quarterback from the beginning of the year (Rattay) as a backup, and SF had to play the game with their 3rd string QB who moonlights as a special teams player. Should have seen the Disney movie coming and jump off the Tampa Bay wagon before it hit studios.

Jeremy—your Broncos looked like Super Bowl Champs today. Jake "The Snake" Plummer spotted again. Green Bay—no comment.

Will say nothing bad about Brett Favre, no matter how the game ended. Awesome idea if it works, bad if it doesn't. Period. The Giants just may be for real and even Houston wins a game. Nice to see you back Tedy Bruschi and now to the final comment on the NFL: I was watching Sportscenter as was engrossed with how Culpepper's season was going to end and then out of nowhere, here comes K. Robinson on a kickoff return and he just gets popped. I've never seen someone get their bell rung so oblivious to it happening. I just remember dropping my jaw and laughing to myself on how hard he just got drilled. Good thing Sportscenter is on 27 times tomorrow so I can see it again!!

Anyway—would love to fill you in on the NHL, but haven't seen a game yet, as OLN is not on my free cable list and anyone can catch the box scores.

Other than that—chilled weekend. Friday marked my "cancer anniversary", as two years ago was when I was diagnosed. It sure feels a hell of a lot longer than that. Oddly—didn't feel well on Friday again and spent the night in a bit of a situation, but came out just fine. Played an absolutely terrible round of golf on Saturday with Korn, Doug Gunderson, and Ross Anderson. I haven't had a good round since I had the transplant and can think of only three reasons why, but not sure which one to blame it on: A: Along with Mark's marrow, I also inherited his golf game. B: The courses just aren't challenging enough to hold my interest for all 18 holes. C: I need a better caddie. I don't know, but something's wrong. Watched "Batman Begins" on Saturday night and thought it was awesome. Definitely the best of all of them. It gets two thumbs up from "Matt's Couch". And Sunday was written above, but I should give another shout out to the "West Wing". If you aren't watching this show—start (even though you will never understand the past—the future of the show is happening now, so you can still ride the wagon).

But—now back to Madison for a few days and go back in on Tuesday. Should be an interesting day and I'll tell more then.

Happy Halloween to everyone and make sure you're giving out the full candy bars—little kids like those houses!!

TUESDAY, NOVEMBER 01, 2005 11:02 PM, CST
DAY 70: 104.0

Why does it not surprise me that I wouldn't make it through October without any problems? I never make it through October without something happening that really doesn't agree with my plans or what I want. October is just an absolutely cursed month and I couldn't care less if they made a new modern day calendar without the month and just added two or three more days to each month and go with 11.

I know—it is November 1st today, so why am I having a beef with October? I'll start by saying that it took a bit, but here I am back in the hospital due to fevers.

It all started on Friday night, just about the time I was supposed to go fishing with my "fishing buddies". While they were catching catfish and bass, I was throttled on the couch with a fever of 104. That is not a typo. I was miserable and cold and shaking and started cursing October with all I could. I took some Tylenol and after numerous wet cloths from Amy, my Pedialyte specialty, and some time, the fever started to come down. After struggling with it for 3 hours, it finally came down and I went from shivering, to releasing the heat from my body, to being just plain clammy and worn out. Fevers just destroy me. Anyway—I'm sure many of you are asking why I didn't go into the doctor, as I am supposed to call with fever over 100.8. Two reasons—last Friday was my two year anniversary of being diagnosed with leukemia and there was no way in hell I was going to spend it in the hospital. Reason two is that I had to golf the next day, which you all already know was a disaster!!

So—seen as fever broke, I didn't call or go in and went about my weekend, feeling like the weather. Now comes Halloween on Monday and the only thing scary about Monday, was how I was feeling. The fever came back around midnight and when I checked it, after shivering myself awake from sleeping, I again was at 104. I got up and went through the same routine as Friday night, but nothing really worked. I went through the stages again and at 4 a.m., was so hot, that I was laying in a bathtub of cold water, which I will have to say, my body turned luke warm. I was all over the board throughout the night and knew that I had to tell the doctor about this one. Good thing I have appointments on Tuesday!!

Well—I know how fevers work, so as I drove into Madison today, I left time to go to my apartment to unpack and then pack for the hospital. I came in for my appointment at 3 p.m. and was just feeling terrible. I told Dawn about my situation and she went right into action (they don't mess around with fevers like I do, which isn't a good thing to do, its just, well, me). I had cultures taken from my lines and from the arm. I went down for a chest x-ray and then back up to clinic.

I then met up with a fellow (who happened to be standing in front of me at the coffee stand when I showed up), Dawn, Linda, and Dr. Juckett. Went over a few things and was told that I would be admitted, which I already knew. Got off easier than I thought I would, so …

As of right now, they don't know what is causing the fever, but I still have one right now. I am on two antibiotics—Ceptazidime, which is infused every 8 hours over a span of 30 minutes and Vanco, which is infused every 12 hours over a 2 hour period, as I am allergic to it and need benadryl pre-med wise (this was the infamous "red man" syndrome, which I had I think back on Day 2 or 3!!). I also went down for a CT-Scan and am currently on a magnesium drip because shocker, that's low.

Anyway—the are treating it as a Pulmonary (lung) infection and as a catheter infection (similar to the infection I had back in Day 2 or 3). Pulmonary looks to not be the case, as chest x-ray clear, but waiting on ct-scan. Hoping it is a catheter infection, as if that is the case, they will be able to just remove my catheter, which would make my life a bit simpler!!

Regardless, I recover very slow from fevers, as they destroy my whole body. Not feeling well as of right now and have barely been able to get out of my chair in my room since I sat in it roughly 5 hours ago. Only move I am making is from my chair to the bed, which is three inches away and could very well take me a half hour to make!!

To end—I hate October, I hate hospitals, and will wonders never cease to find me in the hospital come November!! But—I do appreciate the treatment and care that my team of doctors and nurses here in Madison so quickly and tenaciously provide.

PS—To those of you yet to receive a personal thank you in regards to your generosity, I'm working on it and will just be a few more days behind.

Well—I have to go to bed now as I need my beauty sleep before "Days" comes on tomorrow. Have to catch it all, as you can answer a trivia question that gives you 100 "Days Sony Points", which can be used to buy certain Sony Products—about time my interests start rewarding me!!!

WEDNESDAY, NOVEMBER 02, 2005 11:34 PM, CST
DAY 71: LONG NIGHT—HAZY DAY

I don't even know where to begin, but all I know is that the only positive thing about the hospital, revolves around pain medication and other fancy drugs!! I'll explain.

Last night, Kim walked into my room about midnight to say "HI" and let me know she was going to be my night nurse. She was my night nurse last time I was in, so we chatted for a bit and I told her that I wouldn't be too much trouble. By 6 a.m., that wasn't the truth!!

I woke myself up shivering again about 4 a.m. I was just absolutely freezing, while sweating through my clothes. She took my temp. and let me know that I had a fever again. I can't remember what it was at because I was out of it, but she went right away to get me some Tylenol and covered me with warm blankets. She offered to give me some Demerol, but I refused and said I would be okay in a bit. Twenty minutes later I was still shaking and I asked for the Demerol. She had already ordered it and I'm very surprised how well it worked. I had stopped shaking, but was in no shape to get out from under the blankets and change out of my damp clothes. At this time, I made a plea for some Pedialyte and Kim was somehow able to obtain Enfamil from the pediatric area. It was funny, as the bottles are made so that a nipple can be put on top and a toddler can drink it. She sadly advised me that I would not be getting a nipple with mine and all I could do was chuckle!!

I continued with the antibiotics through the night and was given benadryl before the Vanco, which was nice, as it put me to sleep for a bit. I also had cultures drawn again and all of this took place by 6 a.m. Fun times!!

Well—the normal routine of doctors and other staff came in during the morning, spacing it out just perfectly for me to fall back asleep for roughly 10 minutes at a time. I finally made my way out of bed at 11:30 a.m., but unfortunately, it wasn't to start my day and get ready for "Days".

Dr. Juckett and Linda came in late morning and advised me that what I have is a Staph Infection due to my line. This was the same type of infection I had pre-transplant. They are not sure what type of Staph it is and should find out tomorrow. It is either a serious infection or a mild infection. Either way, my Hickman Catheter would be removed today (which is awesome and miserable at the same time). The mild infection would mean some more antibiotics, pull the line, and should be fine. The serious one would mean they will have to do more lung and heart tests, as its possible that the infection is stuck in one of those areas (can spread to lungs, bones, joints, heart, blood, and central nervous center). This would mean a treatment of 14 to 28 days, depending on what they find. Dr. Juckett is leaning towards the less serious infection, but until it grows in the culture fully, they won't know.

So—that takes us to 11:30 a.m. and I slowly got out of bed and ready to go down to DVI for surgery. I went down to DVI around 12:15 p.m. and had an IV placed in my left hand. These IV's bother me the most, as they are always in the way, you always bump them, and they just plain ache. However, a small price to pay in the long run. I was wheeled into the surgical room and began prep for the Hickman removal. Cont ...

WEDNESDAY, NOVEMBER 02, 2005 11:35 PM, CST
DAY 71: LONG NIGHT—HAZY DAY CONT ...

Funny Story—As I met the team, which included a nurse, a prep person, and two doctors, they advised me that the Hickman should come right out. I immediately laughed and asked what they wanted to bet. It never ceases to amaze me on how little some doctors listen to the patients. They just blew me off and went about their business. After the prep work was done, they gave me some lidacaine around the Hickman site and some IV drugs—they ended up giving me three shots of IV drugs. It took them nearly 45 minutes to get out and they were just pulling and pulling and pulling and it felt like they were trying to rip my throat out. Now it wasn't painful at the time cause I was drugged, but I knew I was in trouble late. Anyway—I couldn't help myself about half way through them tugging and I had to make a comment that they were lucky they didn't bet me anything. Not too much laughter followed, but I laughed, so as long as I was amused, was all that mattered!!

Needless to say, as soon as I came back up to my room, things started wearing off and I have been on 10mg of Oxycodone every four hours and knocked out by the 50mg of Benadryl I need as pre-med before Vanco. I must add that Hickmet was my day nurse and she accommodated me well all day!! (She has always been my nurse in the mornings since July).

So—besides the minor surgery and antibiotic drips, I've slept most the day and am just kind of recovering from things. Hoping that the fever stays away tonight and tomorrow brings good news and I have a more definitive plan on when I will get out and what the regime will be.

Well—my cocktail of oxycodone and a lorazepam has arrived and my bedtime will soon follow.

PS—Thanks for starting the petition to remove October Kari. I appreciate the effort and will do my part here!!

THURSDAY, NOVEMBER 03, 2005 11:21 PM, CST
DAY 72: NO FEVER + HIGH HOPES = GO HOME!!

My goodness did Wednesday night / early Thur. morning sure turn into a mini nightmare!! After I finished my journal entry, I quickly took down my nightly cocktail and was ready to drift away into induced sleep. My hand is killing me and my chest is killing me and all I want to do is sleep. That wouldn't happen for quite some time.

About 11:30 p.m. last night, the vein in my arm that the IV was in, became enlarged and puffy and you could see it from "a mile away" per Kati. As they tried to switch the antibiotics over to saline, the needle must have went through the sidewall of my vein and was just pushing saline into my arm, forming a puffy trench along my vein route. Kati unhooked me and after fiddling with the IV for a few minutes, advised me that I would need a new IV and that Kim would put it in for me. (Realistically it was time to go home time and I'm not dealing with this at the end of my shift).

Kim came in and said she would be a bit and so I sat until 12:15 a.m. Kim came back and tried to place an IV in one of the veins in my upper left arm and failed. It went in, slipped out or broke through the vein, and so now I had an IV in my hand not working and an IV in my arm not working. She took the IV in my arm out for me and called SOS. The nurse from SOS came down around 12:40 a.m. and decided to place an IV in my right upper arm, but only after she shaved the area, which I couldn't understand, as when she placed the bandage, it went where she didn't shave?? I thought maybe I was just seeing things, but that wasn't the case this morning!! However, she did get it to work and I had a successful placement of a pink IV. Sweet.

The night went smooth after that and I crashed pretty good. I was given two rounds of antibiotics through the night and Dr. Juckett and Linda came in just after 10 a.m. this morning. They advised that they were comfortable letting me go with one more round of antibiotics, some oral antibiotics, and if I would call if anything changed. I quickly agreed and was out of the hospital at 2:00ish this afternoon.

I no longer have any IV's, as they were all pulled and now show as nice huge bruises on my hand and arms!! My chest trumps them all and I can't wait for it to heal!! I will be on Moxifloxacin for the next 12 days and should be as good as new!! Also, next Thursday I will be having another bone marrow biopsy performed, which will be another test to make sure the transplant is working and the leukemia is still in remission.

I am relieved to be back home and glad my stay was short, but productive. Should only be a week or two while I recover here at home. Another bump plowed over and now if I can only somehow manage to get my hands on Antonio Gates from Korn in FFL and T.O. in my brothers (I'll pick first and be 8-0) FFL. Stir the pot, but only a little!!

SUNDAY, NOVEMBER 06, 2005 08:37 PM, CST
DAY 73, 74, AND 75: DR. DAVID W. HORTIN

Dr. Hortin was simply just known as "Doc". On Wednesday, November 2nd, 2005, Doc passed on after losing his battle with cancer. His funeral was today in Ann Arbor, MI and I can only imagine what a catch 22 the day was. Celebration and mourning are two opposites that on certain day, become one. I'm sure that is how today was.

Dr. Hortin was the Eastern Michigan Hockey Teams faculty advisor. He was also a successful teacher and lawyer. I met Doc when I was a freshman, just another person finding out how this man could affect a life. Six years later, he was instrumental in my attempt to get into George Washington University for Graduate School in 2001.

In 6 years, I came to be of favor of Doc's passions. From advising on which classes to take, which to avoid, and which would challenge someone looking for one. He was my teacher in numerous law and political classes. He never let me off easy in the classroom, only outside of it. I don't remember him missing a night at "Cross Street" and I don't recall him ever missing any of our hockey parties. I lived in a house that for two years straight, was named best party house of the year. Doc always had the best cup and spot in the house. How else were we supposed to pay him back?!! By the time six years were over, Doc was my teacher, my mentor, my lawyer, and my friend.

The last time I saw Doc was when I left Ypsilanti, MI in July of 2001. Not a memory of school comes up, where his name doesn't pop into my mind. I ask everyone to think of him and to learn more about him by visiting:

www.lifestorynet.com/memories/7853

It will only take a minute to read and will stay with you forever. You just might learn a thing too. It's more important than anything I did or watched this weekend. Sometimes solitude is for a reason and sometimes by choice.

Go Blue.

WEDNESDAY, NOVEMBER 09, 2005 01:41 AM, CST
DAY 76 AND 77: 10 WEEKS, SYRACUSE, AND LUCKY

I am going to say the number 128 and the first person who correctly answers what the number 128 means, wins a free key lime pie. You can e-mail me at Relli11@aol.com to put forth your guesses. You will only have until 10 p.m. on Wednesday evening, which at the present time, leaves you 20 hours and 27 minutes to mull it over. I do expect someone to answer this correctly and will be direly disappointed if it is not. I have two front runners in mind, but am up for surprises. The winner and answer will be written tomorrow night.

And now back to your regular schedule program—today (I am referring to Tuesday, even though it is currently Wednesday—when you need help to sleep and the help doesn't help you sleep, you wind up in my position) marks 10 weeks post-transplant. Hard to believe its been that long—guess time flies when you're having fun. Thanks to everyone who has made the time move quicker. I'm getting better each day post my fever and blunt attack vs. October and expect to be close to 80% when I go in for my 13th (or 14th—need help remembering sometimes) bone marrow biopsy. Like I always say—they get you just strong enough to beat you down again!! Either way—big day … Before I get to the most important aspect of the day, I have a story. There are a few bars in Oshkosh that have poker tournaments once in awhile at them and today just happened to be one of those days. Its something that we have heard of, but never attended. On Monday, Korn and I decided to go and

I called our friend Mike, to see if he was interested. He said he was in and later on in the day Monday, there was a rumor that Lucky was also in. Korn was going to talk to Kramer, so it sounded like it could turn out to be a good showing amongst friends and strangers.

So today came around and the rumor mill had Lucky thinking he might come, but had a few things to check on, and of course, needed permission from his fiance to hang out with the guys for an evening. This is Lucky's way of saying no. After hearing that, I needed to call him and jab at his reasoning. We chatted for a bit and I believe my parting words were somewhere along the line of: "If you get permission and get your gutters cleaned out before its time to come to Oshkosh, I'll see ya then". My thoughts were this: Lucky is going to eat ice cream and pet ponies all night long. Poor Fellow.

When it was all said and done, everyone showed up. Mike, Korn, Kramer, Lucky, and I paid our entrance fee and soon it was time to play. I'll make a long evening short—Mike was done in the first half hour, but used his time wisely to hit the "Monkeys Jackpot" to soften the blow. Kramer went out a few hours later and I followed suit half an hour later. Korn was still in and Lucky was still in, as they combined to form the final table.

I left shortly after and about two hours later, received a call and was informed that Korn missed the money, but that Lucky had won the whole darn thing!! He pocketed a bit over $500 for a few hours of work!! And I am proud to say it is all because of me. Now Lucky did play his cards, but someone has to be the one to convince other people that there is something better to do than what they have already planned—and today I just so happened to be right!! It's awesome when something like that happens to a friend, as its feels like it happened to you also. Can't say I won it, but can at least say I know the "cat" who did. Atta boy my ninja.

As an honor to Lucky, I will take back what I previously said in a journal entry, which references Lucky as "easy money". I now recognize him as a bona fide "player" with mad skills. Props dude and I can't wait for my tricycle!!

PS—16th ranked Syracuse started off the college basketball season with a "W". When one thing ends, another begins. Go Duke!!

WEDNESDAY, NOVEMBER 09, 2005 10:23 PM, CST
DAY 78: DISAPPOINTED

And the answer to the trivia question from yesterday is:

I've decided that due to the lack of response and guesses, that I will keep it open for another 24 hours or until tomorrow at 10 p.m.

There were only a few players and those players guessed quite a few times. I will not share their answers, but thank them for their guesses and making me laugh. Some guesses were on the right path and some were a thousand miles away. My favorites didn't even bother to reply, but a dark horse is seeing the light, although faint!!

There are two people that know the answer and they are no longer in the running for the contest, as I gave in and told them. When someone tracks down your phone number to call you and ask what it is, they deserve the answer. Now they didn't win the key lime pie, but I would gladly buy them a slice of pie anytime and anywhere they want, as that would be the least I could do.

Thanks to those who played today and keep playing. I feel like this is my version of McDonalds monopoly. They always reel you in just long enough for you to get sick (literally—one can only eat so many fries) and quit trying.

As Kenny Chesney sings, "mmmm mmmm mmmm my key lime pie".

PS—A hint: Analytical guesses will lead you on a correct path.

THURSDAY, NOVEMBER 10, 2005 10:31 PM, CST
DAY 79: AND THE WINNER IS ...

First of all, thank you to everyone for your guesses. Some were very entertaining, some where from a different planet, and some came oh so close.

The answer is: From Tuesday, there are 128 days until March Madness Begins!! I referenced the start of the season with Syracuse beginning play and so the mystery is now solved. The winner is: Kevin Morrell. He made the correct guess at roughly 8:55 p.m. this evening. I know—I think its a bit sketchy too, but I guess he would understand my thought process a bit more than most. So—at least the pie stays in house and maybe I will get a piece of it!! Congrats Dad.

Had my bone marrow biopsy today and will know preliminary results on Monday and results of the chromosome marking late next week. Counts still stable—not improving greatly, but not dropping. The 2nd DNA test came back and for immune cells, I am 78% Mark and 22% Matt and for blood cells, I am 92% Mark and 8% Matt.

Its been a long day and so goodnight. 126 Days from today until March Madness. The Countdown to Indianapolis has begun!!

TUESDAY, NOVEMBER 15, 2005 11:52 AM, CST
DAY 80 AND ABOVE ...

Am on another little vacation here to Minnesota, so nothing too much happening, except for the Calgary Flames winning there 7th in a row over the Minnesota Wild last night. Always nice to be in a crowd of Wild fans and having the Flames pull one out for you!!

Results of biopsy and chromosome test will shortly be available. I have a meeting on Thursday with Dr. Juckett in Madison and will know more after that date.

So—will be back on Thur or Fri to leave a message.

PS—Tony Stewart has one more race to go and I think the Packers might have found some magic?? We'll see!!

FRIDAY, NOVEMBER 18, 2005 01:42 AM, CST
QUALITY, NOT QUANTITY

I've tried to start this paragraph for the last week and haven't been able to come up with a clue how. I've been struggling with what to say, how to say it, should I say anything, etc, etc, etc. This is my journey—this has been my adventure—this has been my fate. If I would have had my way, this wouldn't be of any thought to anyone but my family and myself. But along the way, too many people have become involved in the chapters and I haven't quite figured out how extremely fortunate and lucky I have been for that to happen. It's just been so amazing and overwhelming, that there is nothing I could ever do to show my appreciation and in that, my family's appreciation.

To make a long story short, it is with great difficulty that I let everyone know the bone marrow transplant was not a success and my leukemia has returned. Here is where my thoughts and comments fail me and I'd rather be talking about who replaced the Packers last week, how Tony Stewart is one race away from proving my prediction of "2005 NASCAR Nextel Cup Champion" correct, and how dominating Duke was vs. Seton Hall and how the rest of college basketball can fight it out to see who the second rated team in the nation will be after the 1st Monday in April of 2006.

Last Saturday, I stopped taking tacrolimus. As you recall from earlier journal entries, this has been a concern. The leukemia trumps that concern and the point now is to show signs of GVHD to neutralize the spread of leukemia and give the immune system another chance to fight the leukemia. The problem would lie in being able to control the GVHD before it would take over completely. Does this cure the leukemia—no. It buys time.

My father, mother, and I met with Dr. Juckett today in a simply tough conversation. There are options to buy time. Buying time doesn't mean that I will be able to buy time though. There is a recently approved FDA drug called Azacitidine or Vidaza which is being used to treat MDS or Myelodysplastic Syndrome. MDS is a blood disorder which if treated unsuccessfully, turns into AML or the leukemia I am fighting. If it is used to treat AML directly, there are chances it may lead to remission and an outside shot at a cure. I don't need a statistic to let you know the odds of this occurring.

All said and done, my options are to buy time which isn't guaranteed, or let nature take its course. This leads to a discussion on how much is enough? Will a month mean anything if only to be crushed the next month? Do I use my time left to live or be stuck sick and compromised? How is it conceivable that a 28 year old kid with dreams as big as the sky is having to make this choice?

Then I end up comparing quality vs. quantity. When looked at through this angle, my quantity is 28 years. My quality is ageless. I've lived life to its edge and even tested that for 24 years. Why just 24 years? Because I've spent the last four years fighting for a lifetime that maybe I've already had the pleasure of experiencing. These last four years have been a different kind of life and when weeks seem to last years, years become lifetimes. I think anyone who is reading this or supported my journey in any way, is a testament to my life's quality. There is simply no comparison between quantity and quality and to the person who pointed that out to me, maybe just maybe, we've figured out why things are the way they are. I find the peace in that and so should you and so should everyone.

What happens from here—I don't know. For now, I'm doing all I can by stopping the tacrolimus. Everything else is unknown. It's out of my control and in natures hand. I'll keep handling things as they happen and I believe that is the only way anyone can handle life.

I share all of this with everyone not to sadden and trouble anyone or as I've been informed a few times, to make your day go down the shitter. I share all of this because of what you all have shared with me, which is your support, your postings, your e-mails, your time, and a part of your life. Without that I am not composing this and for that, I am honored.

I will continue to post what is happening. Every story has a beginning and an end. Right now, it's just a new chapter.

PS—Make sure to route for #20 on Sunday. It may be his dream but vicariously, it's also mine!!

SUNDAY, NOVEMBER 20, 2005 11:56 PM, CST
YOU HEARD IT HERE FIRST ...

Tony Stewart—aka "Smoke"—aka "2005 Nextel NASCAR Cup Champion"!!!!!!!!!! Nothing left to say. All the hard work I have put into these past 36 Saturdays and Sundays on the couch cheering has paid off. Its been a long, hard season, but watching history just never gets old!! Yeah, yeah, yeah!!

Had a rather eventful weekend—ate breakfast with Amy and my parents early Saturday and then picked up Amy's car she found on Friday—96 Grand AM GT, which Amy refers to as "pretty"!! Got that done in time to see the end of the Ohio State / Michigan game and then catch Duke pounce all over Davidson!! Then on to Dave's ...

Good Story—This summer as I was going through treatments and recovering, I spent a lot of time learning how to fish. Dave, Korn, and I became "fishing buddies" and spent a great deal of time fishing little spots around the valley area. We always used Dave's stuff and at first, Dave had to do everything for us—put on worms, teach us how to cast, how to tell a bite, how to tell what it was before reeling it in, how to tie knots, etc, etc.

Seen as I was immune compromised much of the summer, Dave and Korn had to pretty much do everything for me and all I did was learn how to use the pole. I wouldn't touch the fish or the worms, but had no problem handling the leeches, so that was my only job!! Korn became a quick study and by the end of the summer fishing season, was doing everything by himself, cleaning fish, and whatever. Dave and Korn are now both "fishing masters" and I just tag along!!

Anyway—we ended up finding a bread and butter spot for bluegill, that we fished all summer long between 7 p.m. and 9 p.m. If we got their sooner, nothing. If it got past 9 p.m., nothing. We started slowly, but began to pull out a good amount of keepers each time we went. Kramer decided to join us one evening and that night, we pulled 60 some odd bluegill keepers out of the water. Dave faithfully kept all the bluegill filets after he and Korn cleaned them.

This past Saturday night, we ate the fruits of our labor. Korn, Kramer, Barbiere, Lucky, Amy, and I went to Dave's house (he lives with his brother and his wife) and had a fish fry. All I can say is that we did good. I've never had bluegill before and I would have it anytime!! Can't wait for ice fishing!! (We also watched "Ultimate Fighting 56" on pay per view—good times!!).

That was pretty much the weekend—feeling alright though. Starting to bruise a bit easier than normal and needing some more rest. Good thing we have such a comfortable couch!!

Looking forward to Thanksgiving, as I much rather enjoy Thanksgiving outside of my prison with no bars!! Food is tastier!! Hope all the hunters got a buck, but if not, at least the Packers are on Monday Night!! That's all I've got—Congrats #20!!

SUNDAY, NOVEMBER 27, 2005 09:10 PM, CST
LOOKING FORWARD TO LOUISVILLE:

There really isn't much to report as of the last time I wrote. I have not seen any signs or noticed anything indifferent, that would point to any effects of GVHD. Been sleeping weird hours and sleeping in general a bit more when I fall asleep, but not much else. I have an appointment with Dr. Juckett on Tuesday of this week to check lab counts and a basic checkup. Not assuming much will change and just kind of taking each day one at a time.

I am however looking forward to Louisville, KY this upcoming weekend. My family and a few of my friends are making our way down for a weekend of fun. I'm sure everyone is wondering why Louisville, but that can easily be answered. "Lucero" just happens to be playing Saturday night at "Headliners Bar" in Louisville and I happened to come into a few tickets for the show, so Louisville it is. I see that a nice cold front is coming through towards the end of the week, which will make the temperatures a bit chillier than expected, but hopefully it will be a nice break from reality and up here!!

Other than that, hope everyone had a nice Thanksgiving and avoided being trampled at Wal-Mart for a $3 DVD. Glad to see the "Blue Devils" in top form over Memphis and whispers of Sheldon Williams for P.O.Y. The Packers explain themselves!!

So—hoping for a quick week and a long weekend!!

PS—Still waiting for a key lime pie from Iowa to show up at my apartment!!

THURSDAY, DECEMBER 01, 2005 02:47 AM, CST
AZACITIDINE IT IS

I met with Dr. Juckett on Tuesday and we talked about a few things and I've decided to go ahead and try the shots of Azacitidine.

It is kind of hard to explain the reasoning behind Azac. and what the point is. Azac. sometimes shows the ability to turn immature cells into mature cells. (The Leukemia I have is based on the fact that the immature cells I produce crowd out the mature cells and their function is void). What this entails, is that I will go through four days of shots, have the weekend off, and have another shot. (Starting Tuesday the 6th, 7th, 8th, 9th—10th, 11th off—12th final shot). The hope is for the leukemia to be slowed a bit and give the GVHD a few more weeks to appear.

So far—stopping the tacrolimus has not shown any effects. If the Azac. halts the leukemia and the GVHD shows up and works correctly, it could take out the leukemia. So many intangibles need to work correctly at the right time for anything to work. My counts will drop again, but hopefully not to the levels of being treated with chemotherapy. If they do drop, then I am back in that dark bucket of %$@!.

We will be able to tell if anything is working by the end of December and if it is not working, we won't push the envelope. The worst case scenario is what I am already dealing with. I don't know—maybe I just want to play that last round of golf in North Carolina in 13 days. Maybe nature's just taking too damn long.

On a lighter note—I can almost taste the rack of ribs I'll be eating in Louisville. You always know a weekend is going to be well worth it when there are no expectations. Louisville has no clue what's about to hit it—always leave a mark just to let them know you were there—sometimes you just can't go back!! Ha!!

Will be in touch when I get back and down to Madison. I'm sure I might have one or two stories to share!!

PS—Duke is 6-0 after disposing of "hyped" Indiana. Redick is just unreal. The bad news for the rest of the college basketball nation is that Duke hasn't even run on all cylinders yet. Wow!! I'll take a bet on Duke cutting down the nets—you can all have the rest of America. Send me an offer!!

WEDNESDAY, DECEMBER 07, 2005 06:45 PM, CST
RECOVERING FROM LOUISVILLE!! PART 1

Louisville, Louisville, Louisville—I have had some brilliant ideas in my lifetime. On the contrary, I have had some poor ideas. Louisville however, was definitely a brilliant idea and one heck of a time. The pictures of the weekend are going to do more justice than I ever could in words. I will post a link to them once they are posted online and everyone can enjoy what we experienced!! I'll wrap up a few things for everyone and let the pictures finish the stories!!

We left Appleton on Friday morning in an aircraft that had no heat. To be nice—it was cold. Never flown before in my winter coat, hat, and gloves, but I suppose there is a first for everything!! Due to a delay out of Appleton, we missed our flight in Chicago and were delayed two hours before we were able to take another flight. Once we arrived, as with everyone, unpacking and settling in meant throwing the luggage in the room and heading down to the hotel bar!!

Late afternoon, a few of us took a trip to the Louisville Slugger Museum and were able to catch the last tour of the facility for bat production. It is an amazing process that bat making has turned into and was glad to see it. I ordered a few personalized bats that are being shipped, so I can't wait to see how they turn out!!

After the museum, everyone met up in the hotel bar and planned the evening. We decided on a bar called O'Malleys, which had nothing Irish to do with it!! It was a huge country bar, with two other bars located around it. One was a hip/hop and one was a dance/top 40 bar. There was also a door that led to a different area that was for females only. Needless to say, the females along spent their fair share of time in that area!! As for the evening, we arrived at the bar at 8 p.m. or so and left around 3:30 a.m. (By the time everyone arrived, we were 25 strong or so, with a few starting to slip and some just beginning!!). For a few highlights—The bar is out of stock of a few bottles of Jameson. Some friends have made Louisville acquaintances. Everyone but my dad and I took part in riding a mechanical bull. As mentioned, the girls had some extracurricular activities to see and it turned out to be just a blast!! I ended the night about 4:30 a.m. on Saturday and my sleep was short lived!!

Woke up around 9:30 a.m. on Saturday and picked up a few friends from DC at the airport. By this time, a few friends driving in from Michigan had arrived and were seated at Michael Murphy's—a bar a block from the hotel. Needless to say, the rest of the day was spent there. Spent most of my time catching up with people and introducing people and it was just such an amazing site. The bar took pictures of us for their website and will let you know when they are posted!!

By the time it was to leave for the concert, there turned about to be a total of 36 family and friends. We took shifts in the hotel shuttle to the concert and let that part of the night begin. The opening band "American Princes" was alright and the second band, "Southern Bitch", rocked. Then it was time for "Lucero" and I couldn't wait!!

For a story before this point, I was able to meet the lead singer (Ben) as we were walking in. Amy did most of the talking and Amy and I were able to get our picture taken with him!! Later on in the evening before they were about to go on, Ben came over and talked to me for a few minutes. It was pretty surreal and he promised he would get a song out for the group and I. About halfway through the show it went something like this, "For all the people from Wisconsin, Michigan, Ohio, DC, Missouri and wherever—thanks for coming. This song is for Matt!!". Then they broke into "Slow Dancing" which is my favorite song and rocked it. Phenomenal!! After the show, a few of us were again able to hang out with them and it was all just unbelievable!!

After the concert, a few of us ended the evening at "Freddies 220" and were kicked out at 4 a.m.!! Woke up a tad tired on Sunday morning to say goodbye to family and friends leaving earlier than I!! 10 of us went out to eat and then took the shuttle to the airport, as we were all flying out mid afternoon. The trip home entailed another delay in Chicago and we ended up being 3 hours later than normal. Finally rolled back into Oshkosh around 10 p.m. and soon found a comfy pillow and bed!! Cont…

WEDNESDAY, DECEMBER 07, 2005 07:22 PM, CST
RECOVERING FROM LOUISVILLE—PART 2

On Monday, I met up with Megan Eklund, who had come back to visit a day before we left for Louisville. (If you remember from earlier in the journal, she has just completed her battle vs. cancer and is in the recovery process). We caught up for awhile and then went out to eat at Sergio's before Amy had to work. We just hung out the rest of the evening and it was nice to be able to talk about things that only someone who has gone through cancer and chemo, can truly grasp and understand.

I left early Tuesday morning and drove down to Madison for a 9:00 a.m. appointment. My labs were drawn and counts okay—platelets still dropping a bit and were at 31,000. Then I had my first dosage of Azac. The Azac. needs to be split into two shot doses and so my left upper arm became the first injection site. They didn't hurt at all until later in the day. Now the area is red and puffy and they hurt. Today both shots went into the right arm and they are just starting to bother me a bit!!

Overall, I am rather exhausted, rundown, achy, and sore. Sure it is a combo of the weekend and the shots. Have an exciting week planned of more shots Thur, Fri, and Mon. May be reacquainted with my good friend the couch for a few days, but that's alright. My counts are expected to go down and next blood draw is on Monday. Will be able to tell if someone is wrong before then, but just hoping my counts don't tank and put me back in isolation.

I wanted to thank everyone who made the trip to Louisville and hope everyone had as much fun as I did!! I also want to thank those who keep posting messages to the site. They truly touch me and keep my head up on days it wants to be down. Thank you.

To end, I will post picture links when they come in and try to give a small insight to the weekend!! Next goal—making it to North Carolina next Tuesday without being immune compromised and playing Pinehurst #2 on Thursday!! Simple pleasures turning into dreams and dreams turning into reality!!

PS—Also have plans to visit a few NASCAR Garages in NC, with Joe Gibbs Racing included (Tony Stewart races for Joe Gibbs!!).

SUNDAY, DECEMBER 11, 2005 08:33 PM, CST
LOUISVILLE PICTURES ARE POSTED!!

At the end of the entry, I will post the link to the pictures from Louisville. All pictures were taken by Sara (Todd's Wife) during the trip and set up in an album format on "Shutterfly". You should not have to join "Shutterfly" to view the pictures. If you have any problems, feel free to e-mail me (Relli11@aol.com) and I will send you the direct link and e-mail. Shouldn't be any problems though. I am also going to place the link in the above "links" area. Have not posted one there yet, so hope it works!!

Well the last week went rather quick. I started the Azac. shots on Tuesday. It ended up being a total of two shots each day into my upper arm. I rotated arms each day and sure am glad to have had the weekend off. My upper arms are sore—bruised—uncomfortable—and whatnot. The shots themselves don't hurt, its just the after effects. Kind of interesting—different. Not sure I can say I feel anything different or can tell anything different. Still a bit rundown and tired, but will find out more tomorrow. Have my last day of shots and will be having a CBC done. This will show how my counts are doing, where they stand, and whether I am headed down again. So—nothing on the medical end besides that for now and just trying to make it to North Carolina!!

Had the pleasure of watching JJ Redick and the Duke Blue Devils crush Texas this weekend. 1 vs. 2 was a joke!! I know its early, but if Texas is the second best team in the country, the NBA might want to think about dropping Atlanta down for a few games to make it interesting!!! Long season—I know, I know, but sure great enjoying it!!

Samkon Gado just ran for a touchdown—making the game a tad more interesting here for the Sunday Night Viewers. Good for him. Interesting story—everyone who reads this knows I think

Sherman should be fired and should have years ago. He's terrible. Driving down to Madison today, one of the talk show hosts was going on and on about having Sherman fired. Then he goes, "Who would want the job?". Had to laugh a bit. At least someone agrees with me.

Anyway—here is the link for the pictures. Advice for the day: Watch out for Airplanes in Chicago. Out.

http://share.shutterfly.com/action/welcome?sid=2Qbtm7Jm2YuIg

MONDAY, DECEMBER 12, 2005 11:22 PM, CST
BACK ON THE SADDLE AGAIN

Today I finished my course of shots of Azac. I took the last dose with a shot in each arm, figuring that if they each were hurting, they would cancel each other out while I attempt to swing the golf club a few times. Good idea hey??!! Unfortunately, both of my arms reacted to the Azac. for some reason and I have huge bruise / reaction at the sites. I took a picture of it for proof that even I have ideas that sound solid in relativity, but poor in reality!!

As for my counts, they are down in the bucket again. WBC dropped over 2000 to a whopping 1.8. Hemoglobin down to 10.5. Platelets down to 16,000. Good news is that the shots are producing as advertised. (Won't know if working as desired until later in the month). Bad news—platelet transfusion today. This was a bit different for me, as usually I have my transfusions through my catheter, but I no longer have that. So—they put an IV line in my hand and dripped them in that way. With the blood draw, IV, and two shots, I have four brand new bruises and sore spots!! On the upside, my arms and hands are rather colorful.

They are still allowing me to travel to North Carolina tomorrow. I asked to be cordial and Dawn responded, "If I say yes, you will go. If I say no, you will still go. I'm not making a decision for you!". What this translates into is: Have a good time—Make a Judgement Call—Emergency Rooms in North Carolina stock blood and platelets also!! Already informed Todd that we may have to take a break from traveling North Carolina and visit some of the finer institutions!! I am direly excited to go and can't wait until tomorrow morning. (Secretly hoping the airplane out of Appleton has heat this time though).

I'll be sure to place a few select phone calls on Thursday to a few people, who instead of golfing, will be diligently working. I'll hit some practice balls in your honor!! Will update during trip or when I get back. Hope everyone spends their time wisely at work studying and selecting the Bowl Game winners. Good luck and happy picking.

PS—Arkansas State is overrated.

SUNDAY, DECEMBER 18, 2005 07:33 PM, CST
NORTH CAROLINA, PINEHURST #2, NASCAR, AND PLATELETS!! PART 1.

What an interesting week it has been. I'm not sure where to start, but the beginning is always good!! I will mention that the photo area is updated. Can't figure out how to make the photos larger, so they will just have to do for now!! Anyway, on to the week …

I left for North Carolina on Tuesday morning and arrived early Tuesday evening. Todd was in Asheville for work and met me at the airport. I was fortunate enough to go out to eat with the people in town for the business meeting, met a few people, and enjoyed some quality grouper and crab. However, I found out I don't like grits. Yuck!! The reason I bring this dinner up, is that for desert, I had a piece of homemade Key Lime Pie!! Best Key Lime Pie I have ever had!! After dinner, we went back to the hotel for an early evening. The weather looked to be pretty horrible for Thursday, so we decided to drive to Pinehurst on Wednesday morning and try to get on #2 and play golf Wednesday afternoon.

We got up early and dropped one of Todd's co-workers off at the airport and headed to Pinehurst at 8 a.m. We were able to make a tee time for 12:40 p.m. and then we had to book it. We weren't close to Pinehurst, but we were going to make it!! We basically hauled ass through the bottom of North Carolina, making a few pit stops along the way. We saw the area in a flash, saw some nice areas, some poor areas, a few inmates working on the side of the road with the guard actually pointing his shotgun at them, slowed down a bit to take a picture of "The Rock" or Rockingham Speedway, and as we got closer to Pinehurst, we made a final pit stop on the side of the road, so that I could throw up. Yep—haven't done that in awhile—thrown up on the side of the road that is. Oh well—we were only a few minutes from Pinehurst at this point, so we'll just call it nerves!!

However—we made it. We pulled the car up at 12:15 p.m. and believe it could be record time from Asheville to Pinehurst. They took our clubs for us and we went to park the car. Now seen as we didn't know if we were going to be able to play, we weren't dressed for it. As we parked, we also changed right in the parking lot. Sure they appreciated that, but what are you going to do??!! We put a few layers on and walked into the clubhouse.

Now this place is amazing. You can just feel the emotion and history around you. It was almost chilling. We hit a few warm-up balls and then found out that we were basically the only ones on the course. (I guess they don't like to golf when its 33 degrees in North Carolina—just us "Northerners"). We had Pinehurst #2 to ourselves—are you kidding me??!!

I'll compact our round of golf and say it was simply awesome. Standing on Hole #1, I felt like nothing was wrong—I felt chilled—I felt healthy—I felt relieved. The course was beautiful and shot a solid 95 with four pars, one being a 30 foot par putt from the fringe!! Todd shot an unreal 79, with birdies and pars coming out of everywhere!! The highlight was a 75 foot chip on Hole 9 from the bunker, that just made it on the green, slowed as it came to the downslope, hit the downslope, and made its way right into the cup at the bottom of the downslope. I threw my hands up in the air and started yelling and Todd threw his club up in the air and started dancing a jig!! Funny!!

We took our time, had a blast, and took tons of pictures!! The quote of the day was from me, as we were on a Par 3 which we both parred, but in front of the hole, was a wide bunker surrounding the green and as you walked into it, were looking at about a 10 foot high bunker to get out of onto the green. We each put a ball in the sand and chipped out within 6 feet of the green. Unreal. Then I said, "Nothing like F%&#ing around on Pinehurst #2". We both laughed and I really can't explain how emotional and stirring it was. Many things in life you think about when you are sitting around doing nothing—this will be one of them.

SUNDAY, DECEMBER 18, 2005 07:58 PM, CST
NORTH CAROLINA, PINEHURST #2, NASCAR, AND PLATELETS!! PART 2.

After our round, we checked into the "Carolina" hotel. I have never been in such a fancy hotel before in my life!! I would do it injustice to try and describe it and the room, but I could definitely get used to a lifestyle like that!! We cleaned up a bit and went to "Hackers" to eat. We had some appetizers and a full rack of ribs. Good eats!! Then we went back to the hotel to lounge in the beds, that I swear I would never leave if I had one in my room!!

We woke up on Thursday planning to play Pinehurst #8, but unfortunately, it was raining and cold. An ice storm had gone through where we were headed back to, so we decided to just pack it up and start the drive back, taking a few detours.

Our first detour took us to Lowe's Motor Speedway. What a site. The place holds 173,000 people and the infield holds 39,000 on a race weekend. TV does not do justice to the track, the Speedway, or anything surrounding it. I felt like an ant inside the place. Unreal!! We then made our way to the Hendrick MotorSports Complex for a quick viewing and a we were running out of time in the afternoon, hustled up to the Joe Gibbs Racing Complex. We walked in the door and they had a Tony Stewart Car in the lobby. (See Picture). We also were able to view the garage area (View Picture) and it was just phenomenal. Again—the size of these places are unreal. Just something you have to visit!!

We finally made it back to Asheville around 7 p.m., after leaving Pinehurst at 11 a.m. or so. It was a long drive in the rain and ice, but good viewing. We went to the bar and played a few rounds of golden tee and seen as the pizza placed wouldn't deliver due to the weather, we walked over to the "Waffle House" to eat. If anyone ever watched "Dead Like Me" on HBO, then you will share the same joy and feelings I had walking into it. I left my karma behind at the end of the meal and we were done for the day!!

Woke up Friday morning and Todd dropped me off at the airport. Due to the weather, his flight was cancelled and he had to trek back to Charlotte for his flight. Mine was on schedule, so off I went. I left Asheville on time and then connected in Atlanta. Atlanta sucked. I arrived in Atlanta at 11:30 a.m. local time and left after an 8 hour delay. I was rather nervous, as through the week, I had noticed tiny spots on my body that indicated my platelets were low. I was joking that I wondered if they had vending machines with platelets in them!! By the time I made it back to Appleton, I was in no mood to go to the ER, so I chose to wait until early Saturday morning.

I made my way to the old stomping ground at AMC and was welcomed back with a CBC of very low counts and a platelet count of 8!! This translates to only 8,000, which isn't healthy or good!! (Most people have between 165,000 to 300,000). To make a long day short, I received a needed platelet transfusion on Saturday afternoon and spent the rest of the day sleeping.

So—that was the condensed version of the trip. I make my way back to Madison on Tuesday for more blood work and I'm sure a transfusion or two. But I had a blast, made it home, and all is well as could be. Wouldn't change a thing, except for maybe the well acquainted time spent at Atlanta!! Anyway—Sunday night TV is on and Sunday night Pizza is waiting. Ciao.

WEDNESDAY, DECEMBER 21, 2005 02:40 PM, CST
JUST A QUICK UPDATE ...

Amy and I were down in Madison yesterday and while she was catching up on her sleep, I had another platelet transfusion. Counts for yesterday were: WBC: 1700 Hemoglobin: 9.2 and Platelet Count: 8. Some pretty stellarless numbers if you ask me, but hey, out of my hands!!

Anyway—What this means is that I will be back down in Madison on Friday for more blood work. Seen as I will be going to Minnesota for the holidays, I figured I would skip the Saturday "ER" visit and just get filled up on Friday. I will be back in Madison on the 27th for an appointment with Dr. Juckett, which will see where we go next.

I hope everyone has a happy holiday season and a Merry Christmas.

FRIDAY, DECEMBER 23, 2005 10:33 PM, CST
JUST A QUICK UPDATE 2 ...

Well it has been a rather long and ill week here. Was rather sick with the flu or something on Wednesday and spent most of the day in bed, on the couch, or in the bathroom on my knees. Fun, fun!! Fought off a minor fever and caught up on some rest.

Thursday had me feeling a bit better, so I drove down to Madison. Sounds like I made a wise decision, as the weather here this morning sounded a bit ugly with all the rain and ice. Besides the drive, Thursday saw more couch and nap time.

Today at the hospital had similar results as Tuesday. My WBC dropped to 1.5, Hemoglobin dropped to 9.1, and Platelets held steady at 8. I have been at 8 since last Saturday, which is rather odd. I wonder if 888 has any significance. I'll look into that and let everyone know. Anyway—had another platelet transfusion and had the fortune of having two IV's placed, as the first one decided to slip out of place when we started, which instantly created a golf ball mass of fluid under the skin on my left arm. We stopped that rather quickly!! Not that it mattered a whole lot. All it did was place another bruise on my arm. In a way, it is rather funny, as I have bruises littering my arms, hands, stomach, and legs. I always joke with Amy that I am going to call the cops and have her arrested for "boyfriend abuse". She doesn't find it nearly as amusing as I do, but ...

But—seen as I had a refill today, will be making the trip to Minnesota for the Holidays. Hopefully the snow holds fast and I can make a run at my personal best times. Holiday traffic may come into play, but I'll just have to use the skills I've learned from Tony Stewart.

Again—Hope everyone has a good holiday weekend!!

PS—

Dear Johnny Damon,

You made a name as a Royal. You became a star in Oakland. You became a hero in Boston. You were exciting, memorable, historic, and yourself. Now you are simply a sellout. I would also like to add that you are a *&%&^%*&, *&^$, (*&%&^#%, and a)*%*&. The Yankees of the late 1990's and early 2000's were a team. In fact, arguably one of the best teams ever assembled. Money does not make a team. You will learn that all too late. I can't imagine how it feels to give up your First Amendment Right of "freedom of expression" to collect a paycheck—I guess ask A-Rod, Giambi, and Johnson. I hope you find an expensive barber and purchase some nice things with your $15,000,000 a year because it sure won't buy you another World Series Ring.

Sincerely,
Matthew MW Morrell #11

WEDNESDAY, DECEMBER 28, 2005 07:27 PM, CST
PLAYING CHESS

I'll spare everyone my holiday weekend, but it was a nice time and I was able to see all of my relatives that live in Minnesota and spend time with my family and have some laughs at the expense of my nephew and two nieces.

I also wanted to take a moment and have everyone share a thought for Kari Mattonen, who unfortunately had a relative pass away on Christmas. My thoughts are with you and your family and I'm saddened that the unbidden cancer has taken something from you. May you find peace and solace.

As mentioned in previous entries, I had my appointment with Dr. Juckett on Tuesday. I'll start with the blood counts: WBC Improved to 2.1. (My neutrophil count is only at 164, so the 2.1 is not as promising as it sounds). Hemoglobin dropped to 9.0. Platelets improved drastically to 9. Ha. I received a platelet transfusion and will more than likely be having platelet and blood transfusions on Friday.

The point of the Azacitidine was to lower the counts and buy time for the GVHD. The secondary point was to also lower the blasts of leukemia in my system. Although there are still no signs of GVHD, the Azacitidine was successful in destroying the blasts in my blood counts. That for now is good news. No GVHD as of yet is not so good news.

As my counts begin to recover and the white blood cells begin to grow these next two to three weeks, a new course is going to be tried. I will explain that in a moment. What we are waiting to see, is if in the next two to three weeks as my counts recover, if any blasts again start to grow in the blood. If the blasts begin to appear, well, everyone should know what that means.

If in the next two to three weeks the blasts do not appear, Mark will be kidnapped and released only to find himself hooked back up to his favorite machine in Madison. This time, all that will happen is they will take some blood out of him—I believe enough to transfuse into me over what could be a two to three month time frame. I'll stick to the short-term to be simple for now. In the mean time, I will go through another cycle of Azacitidine shots. At the end of this cycle, they will transfuse a small amount of Mark's blood into my system. This is an attempt to force the GVHD and the outcome would be an onset of GVHD in a few days. Then it would be a battle to control the GVHD and having a million puzzle pieces fall into place at once.

I'm sure most of you are wondering why they did not do this earlier. I can just simply say that the effect of GVHD is hopefully achieved naturally and not forced. I'm crossing off my last option for a cure here and in reality, things do not appear as they seem. There is more involved than I can explain, but the above is a long story short.

So along with the chess game I go. Unfortunately, I have no clue how to play. Therefore, I'm fortunate enough that Dr. Juckett can hold his own!! Yeah—yeah—I'll be here all week.

Go Duke.

MONDAY, JANUARY 02, 2006 10:25 PM, CST
THE FINAL CHAPTER

Just about a week ago, I left Madison with a glimmer of hope and another plan of action simmering in the bag of magic tricks, that has somehow sustained me the past two years and two months. I told my family, friends, and Amy about the good news. I could hear the hope, excitement, and relief in the voices of those I told over the phone. I saw the same emotions in Amy's eyes and the friends I hung out with that night. It is those emotions that have fueled me to fight everyday and to try anything remotely possible to rid myself of my condition.

Friday changed all those emotions. Friday left me with the most gut wrenching task of having to crush all those hopes and make them disappear instantly. I absolutely hate days like Friday and hate what it forces me to do. Excuse my language, but days like Friday and the conversations that follow tear me the fuck apart. I found out Friday the leukemic blasts in my system had risen to 49%. There are going to be no miracles and this story is not going to have the happy ending that has played out in my dreams and in your thoughts. It will however have a different happy ending—a proud ending—an accomplished ending—a loving ending. Only I could be as lucky.

The past two plus years has been nothing short of amazing. The past two plus years has been a miracle. Why? Simply because it has been two plus years and that was never supposed to have happened. I have faced and overcome so much adversity and proven so many "experts" wrong and that is fulfilling by its own. I have only been able to accomplish so much with the support of those of you out there keeping me in your thoughts, through the love of my family, friends, and Amy. Who else can say they have had successfully lived with and fought three major diseases for so long? Who else can say they have had the pleasure of 14 bone marrow biopsies? Who else can say they received a bone marrow transplant from their twin brother? Who else was able to drive from Wisconsin to Calgary, AB for an NHL playoff game at the "Saddledome", take in Yellowstone and the "Badlands", attend a bachelor party in Memphis over the start of "March Madness", travel to Chicago to see a favorite band, travel to Louisville with

40 of those closest to you and see them again, play a round at "Pinehurst #2", and so many other simple pleasures that I don't have room to mention?

I guess what I am trying to say, is that I've been lucky to have not gone through any of this alone. I am lucky to have had the chance to experience so many events the past two plus years, that I was able to put my sickness to the side for a time being. I am going to be lucky enough to not have to see this great journey come to an end alone. I am going to be lucky enough to say final "I love you's" and final "good-byes". Not everyone is so fortunate.

I hope those of you who have been a part of the last two plus years, this entirely different journey of the last five months, and those from as long as I can remember, have learned from me what I was able to learn from you. I hope I have made a difference and made an impact. I hope you have learned that you get out of life what you put into it. I hope you have learned the value of a day. I hope that adversity is no longer a burden, but just a bump on your journey. I hope you have learned to find the "simple pleasures" in life and that a good piece of key lime pie never fails to put a smile on the face.

I will be spending the rest of my time being stabilized with transfusions in Madison until they are no longer reasonable or effective. Hospice will then be involved and nature will take me to the end of the finish line of the life course it has taken me on. I will continue to update the journal for as long as I am able and can't thank everyone enough for how memorable you have made this site and for the support you have shown. Thank you.

I ask that your thoughts turn to my Grandma Morrell, who is presently recovering in the hospital from some health related issues. I ask that your thoughts also continue to be with my family and Amy in the upcoming days and weeks. I'm lucky enough to be able to write my "Final Chapter" and I couldn't ask for more than that. Simple pleasures—simple pleasures.

MONDAY, JANUARY 23, 2006 10:21 PM, CST
SOAKING UP THE SUN---PART 1

I realize it has been three weeks since I have last written. Maybe for lack of not wanting to say anything or maybe just a lack of anything to say until recently. Either way, it's been a good few weeks.

Until this past week, my time has been rather uneventful. I had been spending my Tuesday's and Friday's down in Madison receiving platelet and blood transfusions. With the recent developments, I am transfusion dependent. However, I have been put on Amicar, which is a drug that is supposed to help stabilize my blood system, where transfusions are not needed as often. It has been working, as I am down to visits once per week now.

My last trip to Madison was this past Friday, where I promptly received a healthy dose of platelets. My WBC count has risen to 4.1. This may sound encouraging at first, but in reality, 81% of the 4.1 are leukemic blasts, so that count is steadily taking over, as prior to that, the WBC count was at 2.4, with 64% being leukemic blasts. I am still neutropenic, which has made me wonder sometimes, as I've been doing everything a neutropenic shouldn't be and I haven't been in any serious trouble yet!! Makes me wonder about all the other times when I went into hiding and whether it was necessary at all. Just something to think about I guess!! My platelet count was at 6. Hemoglobin holding at 9.2. My next appointment is this upcoming Thursday, so we'll see what happens then!!

Amy and I spent the 12th and 13th in Minnesota. We drove up that Friday and just hung out at my brother Todd's. On Saturday, Todd and I went to see my grandmother, who is still in the hospital as of today. They finally will be doing a biopsy tomorrow on the spot they found in her lung area. Experience says, "Shit". We'll see.

But back on track here---Saturday night I had the pleasure of attending the Minnesota Wild vs. Calgary Flames. I went with my friends Tim Scully and Tim Klinnert, my mother and father, and Amy and I. Amy and I were decked out in Flames shirts and hats and it was a blast. I don't know of any feeling that is as gratifying and lonely, as jumping up and cheering a Calgary goal in a hostile compound. I did brave the hostiles four times though, in an absolutely 4-1 Calgary trouncing!! Sweet!! Hey Peyton, "Go Flames Go!!".

On Sunday, I pulled a magic rabbit out of my top hat, and Amy and I flew out of Minneapolis airport at 7:20am destined for Hawaii!! My friend Lee from Graduate School is currently in the Army and after serving in Iraq, was stationed in Hawaii. On the Thursday prior to leaving for Minnesota on Friday, I booked the plane tickets, let Amy know, and called Lee and advised him that we would need to be picked up at the Honolulu airport at 3:30pm Sunday afternoon Hawaiian time!! I will cut down on all the details, as I hate to rub 80 degree temperatures in the face of everyone left behind in some of the cooler states at this time of year.

Cont.

MONDAY, JANUARY 23, 2006 11:43 PM, CST
SOAKING UP THE SUN---PART 2

We spent Sunday night in downtown Honolulu at the Hula Grill, having fresh fish while watching the waves crash into the beach. Monday we spent up in the North Shore area, soaking up the sun at a few beaches, trying out different restaurants happy hours and appetizer specials, and walking around without a care in the sunny and breezy weather.

Tuesday, Amy and I had the pleasure of touring the island of Oahu with Curt Harris, the father of Sarah Harris, who is a good friend of Todd and Sara's. We started out in Honolulu and the started a drive up the windward side of the island. We had lunch at the "Plumeria Grill", which is just fabulous. I still can't get over the sight of eating meals outside with the ocean as the background scenery. Tough to beat. The restaurant was at a hotel that had a pool area out back, that played home to dolphins, sea turtles, two sea rays, and numerous other fish. That was awesome!! We continued and stopped numerous times around the windward side of the island and were treated to a great tour of the "sites" of the island and the history behind it. Later in the day, we were allowed to visit a golf course and take a tour of the back nine. This golf course just happened to be in the rain forest area and was simply beautiful. Our last stop was at the Polynesian Cultural Center. Students from islands such as Tahiti, Tonga (learned some geography on this one), Fiji, etc are students at BYU and they perform throughout the day at the P.C.C. in exchange for tuition. At the end of the night, they put on a dance show, which is symbolic of each islands culture. I gave it two thumbs up and would give it my official stamp of approval of necessary places to visit when on the island of Oahu!! By the time we made it back to Lee's condo in Milliana, we had spent close to 12 hours touring Hawaii. Amy and I are very grateful and obliged to Mr. Harris for the time spent with us. ":Mahalo".

Wednesday turned into a bit of a "snafu", but we had a wonderful afternoon with Niles, a quick friend made through Lee and his roommate Dave. We spent some time at Niles's house and he took us to the airport in the early afternoon, where we changed plans and took a direct flight from Honolulu back to Minneapolis!!

As a side note, please keep Lee and his family in your thoughts, as his grandfather passed away on the day Amy and I arrived in Hawaii and he later in the week flew to Albany, NY for the funeral. Time won't forget, but it will ease buddy.

Another adventure and another item crossed off life's "to do" list. I guess I'll keep writing words until the pages stop turning!!

PS--Smuggled in some prime Hawaiian sand in a lemonade bottle for memories and simple pleasure thoughts. Customs never saw it coming!!

MONDAY, JANUARY 30, 2006 10:36 PM, CST
LONG WEEKEND!!

Another week has past by and the tease of Friday and the snow of Sunday, really has me wondering why anyone chooses to live here in Wisconsin sometimes. Sandy beaches, warm temperatures, and calming breezes are only an airplane ride away---but yet someone has to shovel the snow off the deck. Good thing Amy and her bulging biceps and ninja qualities takes care of that (she asked me to put that in here and I'm not sure why, but sometimes you just say, "yes honey"---it's easier!!).

Made a trip to Madison on Thursday and loaded up on a bag of platelets. I can't find my exact blood counts, but they were where they usually are after a week. No surprises. Later that night, went out to the new sports bar that opened in Greenville---"Route 15". My brother Todd was in town for work, so I met him out with a few friends and we did the usual--whooped his butt in "Golden Tee". Ha!! It seems the only time I can beat him at golf, are playing "Golden Tee" or playing for real in Peshtigo, so I'll take my shots when I can!!

I think someone slipped something into my water on Thursday night because I ran into a small Mack Truck on Friday. Felt okay until early evening, when I awoke from my second nap of the day with a tenacious headache. I don't suffer from too many headaches, but when I do, they kick me around at their own will. I can't move my head much, throw up when I try to walk around, and am a crabby boy!! On top of that, I knew I was starting to obtain a fever and the 101.8 reading on the digital thermometer proved my brilliance. I somehow made my way to Walgreens for Tylenol, Pedialyte, tea, and a prescription if things got worse.

I spent Friday night on the couch with a bucket by my head. Amy came home from work that night and was quickly informed of my fate when she set her keys down a bit too loud on the table--sorry!! Spent all day Saturday in bed and moved to the couch on Saturday night, as my headache and fever subsided. Went to bed early and felt a bit better on Sunday.

I was finally able to hold some supper down tonight, along with a key lime pie cookie, so I officially consider myself clear of any problems (after talking with Dr. Juckett of course!!). I'm glad to have escaped this situation, but as always, the fever has sapped me and slowly coming back to "my" par.

Anyway---that was my fun filled weekend and hope everyone else had a better one. I know Tiger Woods and my Dookies did. Back down to Madison on Thursday and will update after that. I've spent a good forty five minutes off the couch here and so I have to say goodnight.

PS--20 days until the Daytona 500. Sweet.

PSS--My grandmother finally was released from the hospital this past weekend and has been moved to a Nursing / Physical Therapy Home. Thank you for your continuing thoughts and well wishes.

TUESDAY, JANUARY 31, 2006 04:07 PM, CST
THOUGHTS AND WELL WISHES NEEDED

Shared with me today was news that shakes you up and again brings the tragedy and trials of life onto your doorstep, only with wishes that the package could just be returned to sender.

I personally have had a few close friends that have fought bravely over in Iraq---Chris Burks (Friend from grade school), Mark Coulthard (My favorite Canadian), and Lee Swietlikowski (Friend from Graduate School). Each one of them has shown me the war in Iraq from their points of view and their battalions mission. They have all made it back relatively unscathed.

Today that changed for myself and countless others. Gary and Renee Neumeyer, their three sons: Andrew, Brett, and Eric, and their extended family, have been lifelong friends of my family. They have two sons serving over in Iraq; Andrew and Eric.

I don't have exact information, but SPC Andrew Neumeyer was recently involved in an incident with being hit by a roadside bomb. In privacy to the Neumeyer's, all I will say is that last we heard, he was being flown to Germany and the prognosis may be better than at first expected. Andrew is being accompanied to Germany with his brother Eric.

Please keep Andrew, the Neumeyer family, and their extended family in your thoughts and well wishes at this undaunting moment and continuing days. Please send them the strength and encouragement that is so direly needed in times such as this.

Thank You.

MONDAY, FEBRUARY 06, 2006 11:00 PM, CST
WILL ADVENTURES NEVER CEASE?!

Congrats to Pittsburgh for your 5th Super Bowl Win. It appears that those who run the NFL, those who air and advertise the NFL, those in Vegas involved in the NFL, and the "phantom" referee squad paid a nice sum in kickbacks, all wanted to see Jerome Bettis retire with a ring. I didn't really care who won the game and thought Mike Holmgren coached an absolutely horrid game, but Seattle should have easily been up 17 or 21-3 early in that game. I'm all for the human element in sports and human error in some judgement calls (see references to MLB Playoffs this past fall), but I think Seattle got a raw deal, that may have severely changed the outcome of the game. But--that is why they still play the game and that is what Pittsburgh did the second half. Sure Disneyland was a blast today and I'll admit I'm glad Bettis left with a ring. Some people are hard to route against!!

I will say the Super Bowl ended a rather long and interesting weekend. Thursday was my second appointment in Madison without having my apartment. I was all gung-ho to arrive at 8am and get the day over with, but didn't seem to drag my lazy butt out of bed until 10am. Started my day at Noon with labs and kicked myself all afternoon. I needed two bags of blood and my platelet count registered pretty much non-existent, so I received 5 units of single donor platelets, which equates to two bags (usually only get one). I didn't arrive home until 9:00/9:30ish pm, so it was a long, long day!!

On Friday, Amy and I made another run to Minnesota. We left when she was done working, 8:10pm to be exact, and arrived in Minnesota about 2:45am. The weather was just terrible from Appleton to Chippewa Falls and I think we both wish we were travelling on a snowmobile, as it would have been faster. We did stop to eat and rest for an hour, but my average time to Minnesota took a huge hit and I don't know if I can recover!!

Saturday morning, we had a meeting at a nursing home and at the end, Grandma has a nose-bleed that we just couldn't stop. The police and ambulance arrived and off to the ER she went. I had the experience of riding in back with her to the hospital and I was rather excited, as it was my first trip in an ambulance without being the patient. My grandma didn't share my excitement, but simple pleasures if you know where I am coming from. The ER stopped the nosebleed with some silver nitrate (can't think of the technical term right now) and so everything turned out fine. Either way, the hospital still sucks, patient or visitor.

Saturday night my Dad, Mom, Todd, Sara, Mark, Michelle, Amy, and I went to see "Les Miserables" in St. Paul. That was my third time seeing it and its still my favorite. Good Times---Long Day!!

Sunday was breakfast and a quick drive back. I was in the dumps, so Amy drove for awhile and then I tried to make up some time from Friday. Made it back in time to play some poker and watch the Super Bowl at Lucky's house.

So--That's a quick synapse of another adventure within and adventure. No Hawaii, but I guess I'll take it!! I guess I'll just keep going and going. It's almost like I am afraid to stop. Maybe I just don't have time to stop. Either way, Duke and North Carolina Game 1 is on tomorrow night and its "Duke" Blue all day long!! Simple Pleasures!!

TUESDAY, FEBRUARY 07, 2006 11:18 PM, CST
DUKE WINS!! 'NUFF SAID!!

SUNDAY, FEBRUARY 12, 2006 11:06 PM, CST
GENTLEMAN...START YOUR ENGINES!!

Denny Hamlin, Number11--Employed by Joe Gibbs--Teammate of Tony Stewart, started his rookie campaign in the 2006 NASCAR Season, with a classy win in the rain delayed Budweiser Shootout. In a race that saw some wild driving, an interesting wreck, and Kyle Busch making some early enemies, the Season definitely started with a shootout. Tony Stewart finished a close second, protecting Hamlin with some nice bump-drafts and veteran blocking for a good 20 laps or so. Thursday brings us the Gatorade 125's and Sunday kicks off the 2006 Season with the Daytona 500. I love Sunday couch-time!!

As for me, this past Thursday was another long day in Madison. For the second straight week I needed both blood and platelets. Platelets again didn't register for a count and my hemoglobin was just under 8.0. WBC count rising as expected and around 6000. However, my blasts make up 83% of that 6000 and I'm starting to feel the effects. My pain medication was upped and I also started taking Celebrex. There are a ton of jokes I could muster on Celebrex, but I'll leave it alone and hope the side effects stay on the side.

Saturday was a fun-filled day as my friend Dave took Amy and I Ice-Fishing. It was the first time I have been able to get out this winter season and was ready for the big one!! We left early and headed out to Shawano Lake. We went on an absolute tear and caught two fish all day. I was happy to break my new ice fishing pole in with a nice blue-gill and we also caught a real nice sunfish that more than likely would have won the tournament going on, but it was caught after 3pm. Amy and Dave share claim to the fish, as it was Amy's pole and jig hole, but Dave was the one fishing. A good combo for such a nice fish and I will post pictures after we get them back. All in all--another fun day on the ice!!

I don't know much else, but for a quick plug, the Post-Crescent has been working on a follow-up story for the past month or so, which will be making its run on Feb. 19th---this Sunday, aka, Daytona 500.

Andrew Neumeyer continues his road to recovery at Walter Reed Army Medical Center, surrounded by his family. Please keep all of them in your thoughts and well-wishes.

Aloha.

PS---Standing behind Dick Cheney is likely to get you shot.

SATURDAY, FEBRUARY 18, 2006 02:51 AM, CST
FIFTEEN MINUTES

I have some exciting news that I would like to share with everyone.

The Post Crescent was interested in doing a follow-up article and what started to be just an article, has turned into a special, exciting, and brilliant package!!

For starters, the article is going to be published this Sunday, Feb. 19th. I learned earlier this week, that it is going to be on the Front Page!! Are you serious??!! I couldn't believe it. It also includes 1 1/2 pages inside and features the article, along with numerous pictures.

A second aspect, is that Amy's Uncle, Bill Glasheen, is a free-lance photographer who works with the Post Crescent and numerous other publications. He has taken the time to follow me on a trip to Madison and also on a few nights out on the town. In which, he obviously has taken numerous photos and audio clips. Besides providing the pictures for the article, he (along with others at the Post Crescent) have put together about a 2 minute multimedia clip, which features his photo's and audio taken. This has already been posted on the Post Crescent site and I invite you all to view it and see how amazing it turned out!!

For those of you not able to see the article for yourself on Sunday, it will be posted online and the address for the post crescent is:

www.postcrescent.com

For the audio link, I will explain how to view it and also post a link that should take you directly to it. Start by going to www.postcrescent.com As you are viewing the homepage, underneath the main photograph, there is a link to "Multimedia". Click on that link. When you are directed to that page, about 3/4's of the way down on the right side, is the multimedia piece. It is entitled "Matthew's Journey". I recommend watching it and then watching it again with the captions turned on, which explain the photos. The direct link should be as follows:

www.postcrescent.com/specials/assets/APCMorrell/index.html

My sincere thanks goes out to Cheryl Sherry for writing the article, Bill Glasheen for the Photos and work on the multimedia, and countless others at the Post Crescent who I have not had the pleasure of meeting, but who have created my "fifteen minutes"!!

As a small plug on myself, I went to Madison on Wednesday this week for two reasons. One was due to the snowstorm that hit Thursday and the second was due to the amount of petechiae. I received a platelet transfusion and was on my way home. A nice short day!! Ha!! I was thrilled that my platelet count even registered---5. Sweet!!

Besides that--battling through the pain, fatigue, and nausea, which has me seeing too much of my toilet. Amy and I also met with home hospice this past Monday and are taking our time on what is best to do. We are leaning at trying to keep me at home as long as possible, with the help of home hospice. If that is too much or not working out, I have the option of a hospice center or an in-patient hospice center in Madison. We've decided to cross that bridge when we run into it.

Don't forget about the Daytona 500 on Sunday and make sure to crank your speakers when the green flag drops. (And someone please try to talk sense into my father about routing for Jeff Gordon---he just won't listen to me!! Ha!!).

WEDNESDAY, MARCH 01, 2006 12:39 AM, CST
THANK YOU READERS AND VISITORS

Thank you to all the people who have viewed the article, watched the multimedia fragment, and offered your support through visiting my site and / or leaving a post for me. I am very honored and very touched.

I know its pretty incomprehensible of me to go past the Daytona 500 and not comment anything. I even went past California. Things have been a bit rough the last few days and so I'll just rant a bit.

If Matt Kenseth had to really ask why Tony Stewart paid a sweet revenge to him after the stunt Kenseth pulled on like lap 28, maybe Team Kenseth needs to start using so some stronger batteries to run their race car driver. Not a big fan of all the complaining already and at least Tony tells you straight up how he feels. I am also wondering how only a crewchief can dictate something on the car without informing the driver, crew, or management. That to me seems impossible.

Otherwise, enjoyed the race until McMurray took out my Fantasy Driver (Kt. Busch) with an idiotic move that he was destined for all day. Oh well---17 more races to move up from the bottom!!

Had appointments in Madison on Wed. and Thursday. Platelets didn't register and my blood was low, so I received two bags of blood and 1 bag of platelets.

Friday, Saturday, Sunday, and Monday, I was dealt a devastating blow to my immune system and myself. I spent all weekend laying around in bed---was fighting a fever from 99.5 to 101.7---couldn't eat anything, couldn't drink anything, threw up I don't know what, as there was nothing in my system--and was just miserable. I didn't even watch the race---unreal!!

Due to the amount of bruises that were appearing on my body, including a huge shiner under my right eye where Amy punched me as hard as she could (boyfriend abuse and J/K), and numerous other areas, went down to Madison today. My counts are completely out of control at the present moment and I received a bag of platelets, some saline hydration, some nausea medication, and potassium. I'll explaining the counts later on this week.

I will be posting some of our fishing photos from a few weeks ago and will try to have those up by Wednesday.

Hope everyone has a good "hump" day tomorrow and thanks again for all everyone has done.

Sincerely,

Matthew MW Morrell

WEDNESDAY, MARCH 08, 2006 04:29 PM, CST

When Matthew began his journal writings he indicated he would share his journey until he could no longer do so... that day has come. Matthew's health has been declining rapidly since Friday, March 3.

We want to let you know that Matthew is resting as comfortably as possible (thank you Hospice care givers), at home, surrounded and cared for by Amy, his family, and close friends. Please keep Matthew in your thoughts and well wishes.

We also know that if Matt could, he would again ask your thoughts and well wishes to go out to Gary Neumeyer and the entire Neumeyer family, who experienced the loss of their brother, Marc Neumeyer, in a tragic traffic accident on Tuesday, March 7, in Neenah, Wisconsin.

Our sincere thanks to all readers and visitors.

The family of Matthew M.W. Morrell

THURSDAY, MARCH 09, 2006 07:07 PM, CST

Matthew's pages have stopped turning...

Matthew Michael Wyatt Morrell passed on peacefully this afternoon surrounded by his family, along with Amy and members of her family.

April 14, 1977 to March 9, 2006

THE FINAL – FINAL CHAPTER

As Matthew's health declined steadily his journal entries lessened, and 2006 brought a tough reality to those who knew and loved Matt. Even many who didn't know him were impacted by his death on March 9, 2006.

On Sunday, March 12, 2006 a steady stream of people touched by Matthew's wit and wisdom, flowed through Kessler Funeral Home in Neenah, Wisconsin. A steady stream of love, hugs, and tears; memories, smiles, and condolences were offered to the loved ones Matt left behind. Over and over during those four and one-half hours, a common statement received from mourners/visitors was 'I/we don't understand/know how Matt handled all that he went through!'

What we do know is that Matthew's journey was not easy for him, and he gave his all to fighting for his life. It wasn't until a final conversation on Tuesday, March 7, 2006 that he gave direction and understanding to just how he did handle all that he had been through.

Matthew asked that an envelope that was on the kitchen counter, addressed to Andrew Neumeyer, be delivered to Andrew. "Please tell him I wrote it but I didn't get it in the mail," Matt said.

The envelope containing the following card and gift, was given to Andrew Neumeyer, who bravely fought in Iraq until he was severely injured by a roadside bomb on January 31, 2006, when Andrew came to spend his final moments with a life-long family friend, and co-twin brother (journal entry January 31, 2006).

2-19-2006

Andrew,

I am truly at a lose for what to say, but my thoughts and well-wishes for you and your family, have been heavily on my mind.

There is no way I can imagine or pretend to know what you are courageously facing and just wanted to share some of what I've learned.

- Take one minute at a time. Slowly move that to one day at a time, but never further.

- You are going to have good days and bad days. Take them both in stride.

- You are going to experience every and any emotion at every and any time. Express everything and do not let it weigh on your soul. Talk with someone, talk to yourself, write it down, or type it out.

- The journey before you will not be an easy road. You will make steps forward, fall five steps back, and move back to where you started. That is okay. Be humble in the failures and celebrate the hell out of successes.

$\longrightarrow$

- lean on everyone and draw support from them. While doing so, rely on and believe in yourself; You will be responsible for your success and know everyone is standing by your side to help and cheer you on.

- It is just fine to be frustrated, to be upset, to break down and cry. You will grow stronger and you will learn to use these emotions to your advantage.

- Make a list of your immediate, short-term and long term goals for your recovery, your personal life, and your dreams. Keep it with you, adjust and add as necessary, and proudly cross them off.

- Find your own "simple pleasure" to get through each day.

- Please call or email me, if there is anything you need or want to talk about. Please extend that to your family. I have numerous friends in Washington D.C. and they will help w/ anything you need or want.

Phone: 920-585-0678
Email: Relli11@aol.com

→

B → Here I've Enclosed
Something Given To Me. I Do
Believe It is Best Suited For
You Now.

It Is A Green Scapular That
Is Said To Have Miraculous
Healing Power.

I've Saved All It's Power
and Energy For You!!

Simply Matthew! Pieces of his heart and soul, along with compassion, courage, honesty, tenderness, and loyalty; shared with a friend, a son, a brother, a soldier, who now is faced with life changing circumstances. Simply words of wisdom.

On March 1, 2006 Matthew's journal entries came to an end. He graciously concluded with sincere thanks to all who viewed the article, watched the multimedia fragment, and offered him support through visiting his site and / or leaving a post for him. "I am honored and very touched" wrote Matthew M.W. Morrell.

Matthew Morrell was dignity to the very end. Quick and wide smiles, hand-breaking hand shakes, that wink and laugh, his voice clever and smart, quietly shouting affection, in confidence, in conversation, in silence, with humility and honor, dignified and very human, wrote R.F. Praefke (see Postscript).

The family of Matthew M.W. Morrell would like to express loving, sincere thanks to CaringBridge, R.F. Praefke, D. Oskin, B. LeRoy, and K. Glidden for all it took to make this book a reality for Matthew. All proceeds will benefit the CaringBridge organization.

The family of Matthew M.W. Morrell would also like to express loving and sincere thanks to Amy Glasheen and her family members, all of Matt's friends, family friends, relatives, co-workers, the many doctors, nurses, caregivers, and strangers-now friends, who shared this journey of Matt's leukemia, key lime pie and simple pleasures.

H.A. Morrell

August/2006